Caring for the
ELDERLY

© John Birdsall Photography

Caring for the
ELDERLY

Veronica Windmill

PITMAN
PUBLISHING

PITMAN PUBLISHING
128 Long Acre, London WC2E 9AN

A Division of Longman Group UK Limited

© Longman Group UK Limited 1992

First published in Great Britain 1992
Reprinted 1993

British Library Cataloguing-in-Publication Data
A catalogue record for this book is available from
the British Library

ISBN 0-273-03871 0

Typeset by Avocet Typesetters, Bicester, Oxon
Printed in England by Clays Ltd, St Ives plc

Contents

10 Problems faced by the elderly 135

11 Getting the best out of life 157

ON AGING

When you see me sitting quietly,
Like a sack left on the shelf,
Don't think I need your chattering.
I'm listening to myself.
Hold! Stop! Don't pity me!
Hold! Stop your sympathy!
Understanding if you got it,
Otherwise I'll do without it!

When my bones are stiff and aching
And my feet won't climb the stair,
I will only ask one favor:
Don't bring me no rocking chair.

When you see me walking, stumbling,
Don't study and get it wrong.
'Cause tired don't mean lazy
And every goodbye ain't gone.
I'm the same person I was back then,
A little less hair, a little less chin,
A lot less lungs and much less wind.
But ain't I lucky I can still breathe in.

Maya Angelou

(Taken from *And Still I Rise*, copyright Maya Angelou 1986
Published by Virago Press 1986)

Introduction

© John Birdsall Photography

The work of caring for the elderly has often suffered from a less than glamorous image both in the caring professions and in society in general. However, with increased awareness of the realities of old age, and an understanding of the way a carer can enable their elderly clients to live a more full and active life, the role is changing.

When discussing the needs of the elderly it is often forgotten that the large majority of the ageing population live independent lives. Even the clients of the caring services about whom we hear so much, are living independently for longer, due to changes in medical technology and in attitudes towards older people. However, eventually many of the elderly in our society will need some care and help to cope with their daily lives. For some the level of support they will require will involve 24-hour, complete care.

Those who have decided to train to care for the elderly are well aware of the possible problems they may face. This book aims to provide a comprehensive overview of the ageing process and to indicate the ways in which the carer may help the elderly to minimise the effects of ageing. Good practice is vital in the care of the elderly and, although good caring practices are involved largely with tasks, the underlying strength of a carer is their positive attitude and approach to their elderly clients:

- Old age is part of the continuum of life
- Even the very infirm elderly have a right to personal dignity
- Self-advocacy should be encouraged in all recipients of care
- Be aware of good and bad practice in other carers
- If you are uncertain about the reasons for doing anything in the care situation, question it – greater knowledge brings greater understanding
- Be aware of your own behaviour and attitudes, and the effect it has on others. Be willing to change if necessary
- Everyone, regardless of age, race or culture is an individual and should be treated as such.

The text is designed to develop the knowledge of students studying the BTEC First Certificate and Diploma in Caring and the relevant City and Guilds schemes.

How to use this book

Caring for the elderly is a complex issue which this book aims to make clear. The topics examined in each chapter are inter-related so should always be read in the light of each other. The assignments at the end of the chapters involve a variety of tasks which are aimed at reinforcing the learning elements of chapters while placing the subjects discussed in a wider social context. Researching the provision for the elderly in your local area, for example, gives a more complete understanding of the situation than can be gained from purely academic research.

1 Attitudes towards the elderly

© John Birdsall Photography

When people are asked what their attitude is towards becoming old their answers are frequently negative. It is difficult to find someone who talks about ageing with any enthusiasm; for most it is something to be put off and dealt with nearer the time.

It is not surprising that this attitude has developed, considering the images which surround old age in western societies.

Media and cultural influences on perceptions of old age

From their early years children are presented with negative images of the elderly. Although there are some positive elderly characters in traditional children's literature such as the fairy godmother, these are far outweighed by wicked and frightening old characters – like the wicked old witch of so many fairy tales. These traditional forbidding representations of the elderly have been reinforced in films, cartoons and stories for children over many years, although more recently efforts have been made to redress the balance in children's fiction, with elderly men and women being included in ordinary everyday situations.

Even as we grow older there are still plenty of characters to be found who build on the negative childhood images of old age. Old women, in particular, are frequently depicted as evil and demented.

In the 1950s a new style of music became popular in the USA – rock 'n roll – music by the young for the young. The music spread and the cult became a youth culture. Much of pop music since the 1950s has

© Emma Flack

celebrated youth, and for the young, ageing became something to be avoided.

Without the financial responsibilities of home and family, many young people were free to spend their money as they chose. The fashion and media industries were not slow to see the potential profit this new market offered and began increasingly to cater for the young. Clothes, records, films, food and so on were produced to feed the tastes of this new youthful market, and the advertisers targeted them in their commercials, using only young men and women as models. On the rare occasions the elderly were presented in the media, their roles tended to be minor or passive and often merely stereotypes of frail old grannies or stubborn, silly old men. It would seem that, by concentrating on youth, the aged and elderly have been either ignored or they, and their views and opinions, have become objects of ridicule. The law tells them they can no longer work; society suggests they shouldn't have sex; the media tells them they are no longer attractive.

This stream of negative impressions of the elderly has a strong cumulative effect both on the self-esteem of the elderly and on the way in which they are perceived by the rest of the population. Our culture does very little to help promote a positive image of old age and one result of this is prejudice and discrimination towards the elderly – ageism. Ageism has not always existed; it is a relatively modern and largely western phenomenon.

It is vital that everyone involved in caring for the elderly is aware and sensitive to the needs of their elderly clients as individuals – people with desires and needs just like the rest of the population.

The extended and the nuclear family

In the extended family many generations live either under one roof or in close proximity to each other. Such a family structure can be found in many cultures and tends to be more home-orientated, with more traditional roles for the men and women of the family. The women generally run the home, and care for the children and the sick, while the men work and provide for the family. The elderly are, therefore, included in the day-to-day running of the family and are not seen as a burden or liability.

In the industrialised western world the traditional extended family has largely been replaced by the nuclear family. This is where a couple, and their children if they have any, live under one roof. The couple no longer live with their parents and have often moved to a different area in pursuit of work. With the increase in the number of divorces, it is not unusual for nuclear families to have only one parent living in the family home.

As the parents of the nuclear couples grow older there are usually few problems. Travel is relatively simple so regular visits can be made and improved health care means that the average elderly person can expect good health, and therefore independence, for most of their life. If, however, the elderly person is no longer able to cope, for one reason or another, problems may develop. The nuclear family is not geared to coping with the needs of an elderly person for a variety of reasons:

- Modern houses are small.
- Increasing mobility means that the family may live far away from the elderly person and this raises many questions – for instance, whether it is fair to the elderly person to move them away from familiar surroundings and friends.
- The traditional carer, the woman of the family, may have a career of her own and be unwilling or unable to give it up to stay at home.
- The elderly person may feel guilty about being a burden to the family, knowing the situation – an attitude reinforced by the media, State provision for the elderly and cultural attitudes.

The effects of modern life on the elderly

Because modern industrialised society operates around the nuclear family, the elderly tend to be left out in the cold. Some of the reasons for this are:

- People are encouraged in their youth to achieve a good career with prospects and to invest wisely for their old age. Then, at retirement age, they are suddenly no longer seen as a useful part of society. They frequently feel undervalued and redundant.
- Society encourages independence – the elderly person needing help often feels very guilty.
- Everyday life is not geared towards the needs of the elderly – shopping facilities being sited out of town and the disappearance of much accessible public transport are just two examples of this.
- In the past the elderly were cared for by their family, usually a daughter. Today, many people, particularly women, have higher personal and career aspirations, and an increasing number have greater responsibility for the financial support of home and family than ever before. Many would be unwilling – or unable – to commit themselves to caring for an elderly relative.
- There is a general belief that the State will support the elderly in society. Not only did the elderly themselves contribute to the National Insurance fund when they were working, workers continue to have money deducted from their pay to fund state provision and pensions.

Modern industrial society tends to undervalue the elderly because they are not seen to have a relevant role to play, i.e. they don't earn money like the majority of the population do. As a result, people tend to ignore their needs and their opinions. The elderly in less-developed countries where the extended family still exists, however, do not feel undervalued as they still have a useful role to fulfil and their opinions are valued for their wisdom and experience.

The implications of our attitudes towards the elderly

Overall, these factors result in a general feeling that growing old is not something to look forward to. The vast majority of the elderly population live healthy and independent lives, but this is often overlooked for the following reasons:

- they are not discussed in the media
- they are not factors in political debates
- they are not more likely to be Health Service patients
- they are not more likely to be Social Services clients.

Society's attitudes towards the elderly are partly reflected in the way the caring services are run. Here are some examples, but there are many more.

- Working with the elderly is still one of the less popular areas of medicine.
- Care assistants for the elderly have a low status both inside and outside the profession.
- We still read in the press of the elderly being abused in residential homes. Perhaps it is a sad indictment of society that we don't read about the good carers.
- Many would argue that services for the elderly are grossly underfunded.
- Politicians seem to give a low priority to the needs of the elderly population.
- Residential homes for the elderly are being closed down as community care is introduced. Many would argue that there are not adequate resources to care for the elderly being returned to the community.
- Training for those caring for the elderly has been a low priority, although there are plans to improve this situation.

People either working with the elderly, or considering doing so, need to be aware of the issues raised in this chapter. It is vital that we make positive efforts to see old age as part of the continuum of life, and not as something tagged on the end – the elderly are not a different species.

This might seem a difficult task for those working with the elderly who do have problems, when it may become easy to forget that the majority of the elderly live independent and satisfying lives without needing the help of a carer. It may also be difficult to bear in mind when reading this book which is written for people working with the less able elderly. However, the carer does need to develop an awareness of these issues when developing their caring model.

Key issues – a summary

- Society does little to promote a positive attitude towards ageing. The elderly are often stereotyped as being cantankerous, stubborn and forgetful.

- Advertising and the media promote youth culture as it promises big profits to the fashion and music industries. As a result, the elderly tend to be ignored.

- The elderly are not encouraged to be fashion-conscious or sexually active. These activities are seen as belonging to younger people.

- Enforced retirement may create a feeling of uselessness.

- Poor attitudes towards the elderly are the root cause of ageism – discrimination on the basis of age.

- The extended family tends to give rise to fewer identity problems for elderly family members who feel valued and are respected.

- The nuclear family is less able to cope with the needs of a dependent elderly relative for the following reasons:

  - smaller houses
  - increased mobility
  - increased aspirations of women
  - Welfare State provision.

- Modern society tends to ignore the needs of the elderly in the following ways:

  - they receive less respect as they are not earning money
  - they do not work, so they have a less well-defined role to play
  - shopping facilities becoming less accessible
  - public transport is diminishing.

- It is easy to forget that the vast majority of the elderly live independent lives because society only gets to hear about the elderly with health, social or financial problems.

- The services caring for the elderly tend to have a low status, both inside and outside the profession. Public awareness needs to be raised in order to improve funding and training.

- People working with the elderly need to devise a philosophy that treats the elderly with dignity.

Assignment 1   Society's view of the elderly

TASK 1:
CHILDREN'S FICTION

Old people, particularly women, are often portrayed as being wicked and bad in children's fairy tales. More recent stories have tended to be more realistic and sympathetic. Visit your local library to do the following research:

(*a*) Find three fairy tales and three modern stories which contain elderly characters.

(*b*) For each, jot down notes about:
  • whether they are male or female
  • their role
  • their appearance
  • whether they are good or bad.

(*c*) Discuss the similarities and/or differences between the approaches of the old and the new.

You may like to do some follow-up research on some children. There are two ways you can do this:

• You can devise a few questions beforehand that aim to find out whether their attitudes towards the elderly are influenced by what they read.
• You could read some of the old and new stories to them and ask questions about the elderly characters.

TASK 2:
ADVERTISING

Advertising generally uses younger people to promote its products. When elderly people are used, it is often in a stereotypical role.

Collect a series of about ten advertisements, from both television and magazines, that includes elderly people. Discuss the aim of each advert and the role of the elderly person.

Are there any conclusions you can draw?

TASK 3:
DRAMA AND
LITERATURE

Discuss and list any films, television programmes, books and plays that portray old age in a positive light (i.e. not as dependants, grandparents or frail and sick).

Why do you think writers are reluctant to make older people the central character?

TASK 4:
SEXUALITY AND THE
ELDERLY

The elderly are actively discouraged from demonstrating their sexuality by society's disapproval. Women, in particular, are encouraged to disguise or hide their age because they might be thought to be 'past it'.

Why do you think society disapproves of the elderly having sexual feelings and how does it show its disapproval?

**TASK 5:
AGEISM**

Ageism, like sexism and racism, is very destructive. List as many instances of ageism as you can. The following headings may help you:

- social aspects
- sexual differences
- the law
- culture
- language.

When you have completed your list, consider what society can do to reduce the effects of ageism. Note down your ideas under the headings of:

- education
- legislation and codes of practice.

**TASK 6:
FAMILY
STRUCTURES**

Find out about the nuclear and the extended family. To help your research, you may like to put your findings under these headings:

- a definition of the two terms
- where you would find nuclear and extended families
- the findings of research carried out by:
  —Rosser and Harris
  —Young and Wilmott
  —A Oakley
- a general conclusion explaining:
  —why the extended family is dying out in industrialised societies
  —why the nuclear family is developing
  —the effects of these changes on the elderly.

**TASK 7:
AGENCIES
SUPPORTING THE
ELDERLY**

In Britain, apart from family and friends, help for the elderly with health or social problems is also offered by:

- the local authority
- central government
- voluntary agencies
- the private sector.

In groups, find out the following:

- a definition of the terms
- how the funding of each differs
- three examples of each
- the advantages and disadvantages of each for the elderly and their families.

TASK 8:
PRACTICAL LIVING
PROBLEMS

Shopping centres are being built out-of-town and public transport is suffering from a lack of funding. Can you think of any other factors that make everyday life more difficult for the elderly?

TASK 9:
STATUS OF CARERS

In groups, discuss the problem of low status among those caring for the elderly. In your discussion, consider:

(a) how the low status developed;
(b) examples from the workplace;
(c) suggestions on how to raise the status of carers.

2 Sociological influences on the elderly

© John Birdsall Photography

We have looked at how the elderly in our society are victims of stereotyping and preconceptions, so we should now be aware of how important it is to promote a positive approach to caring for the elderly; to encourage proaction rather than reaction.

To help instil this belief in the carer, we shall look at other factors affecting the elderly.

Social differences

Society is divided up into categories that generally put people into hierarchies – this is called social stratification. In the UK people are categorised according to their social class while other cultures use different criteria and systems. In India, for example, members of the Hindu faith are classified according to the caste system. As well as categorising people, social stratification can also separate them. The caste system for instance allows little contact between the castes and there is no movement up or down the caste hierarchy – people stay in the caste they were born into for their entire lives. Although the British class system is not so rigid, it can still have a strong influence over our lives. Other influences are gender, race and family history.

Social class, gender and race all need to be considered by policy makers when they are determining future needs of the elderly as these three elements form the basis of the statistical trends which are vital to informed planning. Though many people are wary of the accuracy of many statistics, they are one of the few ways of predicting future demand and so appropriate responses to client need.

Social class

The Government's statistical department divides the population into five social classes.

Social class 1
Doctors, lawyers, judges, high-level managers, university lecturers etc.

Social class 2
Lower level professionals such as teachers, small business persons, airline pilots, middle managers etc.

Social class 3A
Whitecollar workers such as clerks and secretaries, shop assistants etc.

Social class 3B
Skilled manual workers such as bricklayers, electricians, hairdressers etc.

Social class 4
Semi-skilled workers such as post office workers, farm workers etc.

Social class 5
Unskilled workers such as cleaners, porters and manual labourers etc.

Statistically is has been found that the higher the social class, the more likely it is that the person will:

- receive a better education
- live longer
- be generally healthier
- have a higher standard of living

- not be in trouble with the law
- not live in poverty
- earn more money
- own their own house
- invest in their future
- have leisure activities
- follow an exercise programme
- demand their rights.

Gender

Whether a child is born a boy or a girl affects their future lives to a great extent. A woman's place in society is a very controversial issue and has provoked decades of passionate debate which has led both to changes in the law and to a number of sexist jokes.

The influence of gender is very strong, and it has been accepted that women have suffered discrimination in many areas of society for centuries. Efforts continue to be made in education, in law and by women themselves to achieve equality of opportunity, and redress the balance.

Physically, gender has some bearing on how long we live. Statistically:

- women tend to live longer than men;
- more male babies are miscarried than female;
- males suffer from more gender-linked disorders such as haemophilia, colour blindness, and Duchenne and Becker type muscular dystrophy – although females can carry the affected genes.

Race

Racial discrimination, despite legislation designed to stop it, is still a fact of life in the UK. Ethnic minorities in Britain are, like the lower social classes, more likely to have problems in getting jobs, leading to a higher incidence of poverty, ill-health, poor housing and other poverty-related disadvantages.

Race-related diseases, such as sickle-cell anaemia, thalassaemia and rickets, need to be carefully monitored. Health service workers also need to be aware of cultural differences such as language barriers and religious beliefs.

Family history

Certain physical and mental health disorders are thought to be partly influenced by heredity. This stresses the need for medical staff to check through their patients' medical notes and, where possible, to discuss family medical backgrounds with patients and families.

Demographic influences

Demography is the study of populations, and can be used to help the health and social services estimate the number of clients they will be dealing with in the future. Policy makers must take note of demographic changes when planning care provision for the elderly.

Life expectancy statistics are useful when estimating the size of a population group in the future (*see* Fig 2.1). Similarly, when attempting to anticipate possible areas of care provision that may be required in the future, statistics relating to causes of death over a range of time may give indications of trends in the prevalence of various diseases as well as life expectancy changes (*see* Fig 2.2).

	Males			Females		
	1901	1989	2001	1901	1989	2001
Expectation of life[1]						
At birth	45.5	72.8	73.9	49.0	78.4	79.8
At age:						
1 year	53.6	72.4	73.4	55.8	78.0	79.3
10 years	50.4	63.7	64.6	52.7	69.2	70.5
20 years	41.7	53.9	54.8	44.1	59.4	60.6
30 years	33.8	44.3	45.1	35.9	49.5	50.8
40 years	26.1	34.8	35.7	28.3	39.8	41.0
50 years	19.3	25.6	26.7	21.1	30.4	31.6
60 years	13.3	17.4	18.5	14.6	21.7	22.7
70 years	8.5	10.9	11.9	9.2	14.2	15.1
80 years	4.9	6.2	6.9	5.3	8.2	8.8

1 Further number of years which a person could be expected to live.

Fig 2.1 Expectation of life: by sex and age (United Kingdom)
(*Source:* Government Actuary's Department)

The numbers of elderly in a population are affected by many factors:

- improved living conditions, promoting a longer, healthy, independent life
- smoking and alcohol, leading to a reduced life expectancy
- higher standards of medical care and improved medical technology increasing life expectancy
- diet – a healthy diet can improve life expectancy while a poor diet can lead to various health disorders
- wars cause increased death rates, particularly among young men, leading to a fall in the birth rate.

There are also regional and local variations caused by:

- people of retirement age moving to a popular retirement area, or
- younger people moving out of an area and leaving the older people behind.

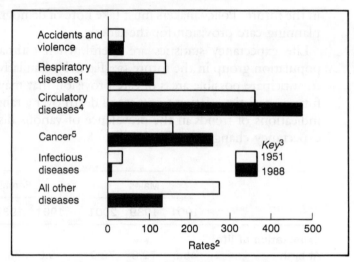

1 On 1 January1986, a new certificate for deaths within the first 28 days
  of life was introduced in England and Wales. It is not possible to assign
  one underlying cause of death from this certificate. For the sake
  of constituency figures exclude deaths under 28 days.
2 Per 1,000 deaths.
3 Care should be taken when comparing 1951 with 1988 because of the
  change in coding procedure (in 1984). The effect of this has been
  to reduce numbers of deaths assigned to respiratory causes.
4 Includes heart attacks and strokes.
5 The figures for cancer include both malignant and benign cancers.

Source: Office of Population Censuses and Surveys: General Registrar
Office (Scotland): General Registrar Office (Northern Ireland)

Fig 2.2 Deaths[1] by selected causes, 1951 and 1988

(Taken from *Social Trends 20*. Reproduced by kind permission of HMSO. Crown copyright 1990.)

It is therefore a complicated task to try and predict future needs, but
without projected numbers, provision would be inadequate and unable
to cope with changes in demand.

Key issues – a summary

- Social stratification is used to categorise people, but it can also be used
  to separate them into superior and inferior groups.

- Social class influences our standard of living. The higher your social
  class, the more likely you are to be well-off and healthy.

- Women and men have differing needs, and these must be considered
  by the caring services.

- The carers of the elderly from ethnic minorities need to be aware of
  additional problem which may arise due to language, cultural and
  religious differences.

■ The government, local authorities, Regional Health Authorities and the social services all attempt to make policy decisions based on projected facts and figures.

Assignment 2 Sociological factors

TASK 1:
SOCIAL CLASS

Find out more about social class by researching in the sociology section of your library.

Your research should include:

(a) the various ways of defining social class
(b) how social class affects:
  ● education
  ● health
  ● living standards.

When you have completed your research:

(a) consider the ways in which social class affects the elderly in terms of:
  ● living standards
  ● provision of community care
  ● health.
(b) discuss the implications of your findings for carers.

TASK 2:
WOMEN'S ISSUES

Women have been striving for equality of opportunity for some time, and laws have been passed in an attempt to improve the position of women in society. Find out about the following laws:

● Married Women's Property Act 1882
● Matrimonial Proceeding and Property Act 1970
● Various changes in the divorce laws
● Sex Disqualification Act 1919
● Equal Pay Act 1970
● Sex Discrimination Act 1975
● Changes in women's voting rights in 1918 and 1928.

The law, together with the Equal Opportunities Commission and various women's pressure groups, has helped to improve women's role in society. What effects do you think these changes have had on today's elderly?

TASK 3:
LIFE EXPECTANCY

Women tend to live longer than men. List the implications this has on the provision of care for the elderly.

TASK 4:
CULTURAL
AWARENESS

Discuss the factors that need to be considered when catering for the needs of the elderly from other cultures.

TASK 5:
DEMOGRAPHIC
FACTORS

The projected numbers of the elderly in the population are affected by factors such as war, smoking and alcohol consumption, medical care available, diet and living conditions.

TASK 6:
STATISTICS

Outline what you consider to be the dangers of relying too heavily on statistics.

3 Physical and mental aspects of ageing

© John Birdsall Photography

The body and mind of an individual change throughout life, so why is there so much interest in the changes associated with old age? The likely answer is that old age is one of the milestones in our lives – one of the 'seven ages of man'. These ages are babyhood, childhood, adolescence, young adulthood, young middle-age, old middle-age and old age. Many artists and writers have been preoccupied with these milestone ages and the rites of passage between them, probably because they are recognised as turning points in all our lives. Old age is simply the last phase in a continuum which begins with birth.

What is ageing?

Society tends to see ageing as a chronological process. At the age of 60 for a woman, or 65 for a man, they are seen as no longer useful in the workplace. Whether or not individuals are capable, fit and healthy is almost irrelevant; they are obliged to leave work and retire.

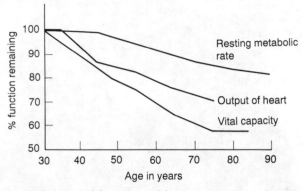

Fig 3.1 Loss of function with age

Clearly, it is administratively easier to see ageing in this way, but there is far more to the ageing process than the simple passing of time. Just as the way food is stored and cared for can affect its shelf life, so there are major factors which can affect how fast a person ages. These influential factors include:

- environment
- heredity
- when the individual was born
- ethnic group
- social class
- gender.

There have been numerous theories put forward to attempt to explain why human beings age; a list of some of them follows.

Some biological theories of ageing

- **The biological clock**
  Each of the more advanced forms of life on earth has an average lifespan. This theory suggests that the time taken from birth to death is pre-programmed, with tissue cells dying off at a set time.

- **The 'Hayflick limit'**

  Research by Hayflick found that tissue cells can only reproduce up to 40 or 50 times, and after this they die. Theoretically, this may control our lifespan.

- **The auto-immune theory**

  The body's immune system protects us from disease. This theory suggests that in old age the immune system not only becomes less efficient at fighting disease, but may also turn on itself.

- **Ageing of the muscles and skeleton**

  The connective tissue in the body loses its elasticity and becomes stiff. This causes some of the more apparent signs of ageing such as the thinning of skin and bone mass, loss of height, stiffening of the joints and muscles and loss of elasticity in the lungs.

- **Error accumulation**

  This theory suggests that the longer a cell exists, the more likely it is that errors will occur. A faulty cell will, in time, cause a malfunction of the body system, leading to eventual death.

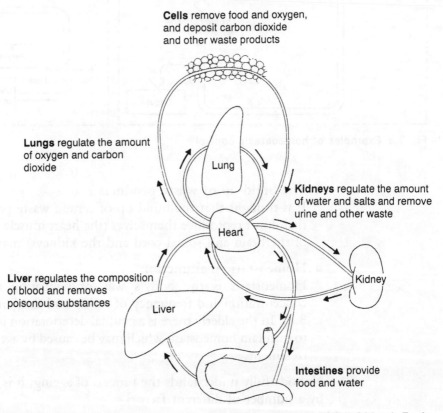

Cells remove food and oxygen, and deposit carbon dioxide and other waste products

Lungs regulate the amount of oxygen and carbon dioxide

Kidneys regulate the amount of water and salts and remove urine and other waste

Liver regulates the composition of blood and removes poisonous substances

Intestines provide food and water

Lung
Heart
Kidney
Liver

Fig 3.2 Some of the processes involved in the homeostasis of blood. Each process is controlled by its own particular nerves and hormones

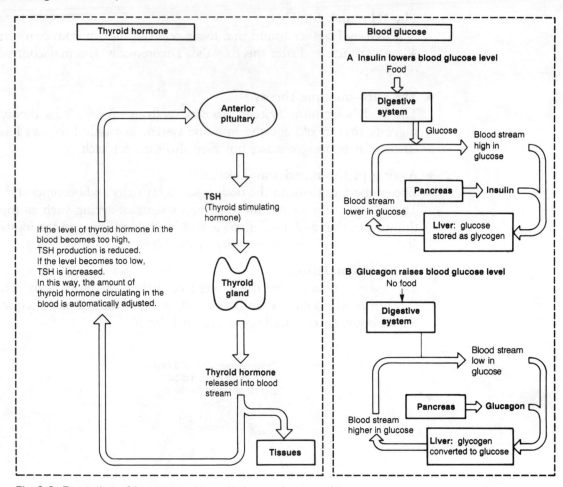

Fig 3.3 Examples of homeostasis control

- **The build-up of waste products**

  It is thought that the build up of certain waste products in the cells that don't reproduce themselves (the heart muscle, the nervous tissue of the brain and spinal cord and the kidneys) may be harmful.

- **Homeostatic malfunction**

  Homeostasis is the body's way of regulating temperature, fluid concentration and frequency of eating and drinking (*see* Figs 3.2 and 3.3). In the elderly there is a gradual deterioration in the body's ability to maintain homeostasis which may be caused by ageing, disease or drug treatment.

  Nobody fully understands the process of ageing; it is clearly determined by a number of different factors.

Physical changes

The changes in the body's internal functions caused by ageing affect the function and appearance of the body. These changes are outlined below.

Visible changes
- The hair thins and becomes grey as it loses its pigmentation.
- The skin becomes drier and less elastic, causing wrinkling. There may be small patches of brown pigmentation.

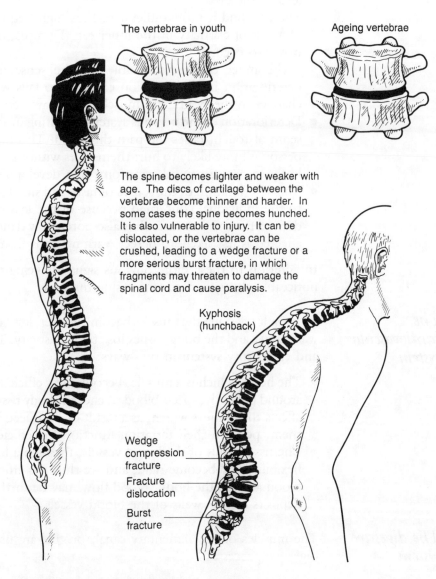

The vertebrae in youth

Ageing vertebrae

The spine becomes lighter and weaker with age. The discs of cartilage between the vertebrae become thinner and harder. In some cases the spine becomes hunched. It is also vulnerable to injury. It can be dislocated, or the vertebrae can be crushed, leading to a wedge fracture or a more serious burst fracture, in which fragments may threaten to damage the spinal cord and cause paralysis.

Kyphosis
(hunchback)

Wedge
compression
fracture

Fracture
dislocation

Burst
fracture

Fig 3.4 What happens as the spine ages

- The muscles become weaker and less flexible, and eventually waste away.
- Bones become lighter and more brittle, and joints may become arthritic, affecting posture. (*See* Fig 3.4.)
- The nervous system becomes less efficient, often resulting in a loss of short-term memory and an increase in reaction time.

The senses

The senses become less accurate as the physical deterioration experienced in ageing progresses.

- In middle-age, the eyes tend to become longsighted, making it difficult to focus on close objects. This is caused by a loss of elasticity in the lens of the eye.
- The ears find it more difficult to hear high-frequency noises because of a loss of elasticity in the inner ear. Tinnitus, or noises in the ear, may also occur.
  The inner ear is responsible for the sense of balance and any deterioration in this function can lead to falls which, coupled with changes in the bones and muscles, can have serious consequences.
- Deterioration of the nervous system, resulting in an impairment of the sense of touch, raises the pain threshold. This means that an elderly person is more likely to hurt themselves without realising it, and is less likely to notice painful symptoms of a developing illness.
- The deterioration of the senses of taste and smell is not only annoying to the individual concerned because of the loss of pleasure formerly derived from these senses, it is also potentially dangerous as the person affected is less likely to detect warning signs from gas or fumes.

In addition to these more obvious signs of ageing there are other, less noticeable changes, occurring inside the body.

The cardiovascular system

As a result of ageing the muscles become weaker, less flexible and eventually waste away and the body tissues lose their elasticity. This affects the heart and circulatory system in two ways:

- The heart, which is a muscle, becomes less efficient at pumping blood around the body, so less blood reaches the body tissues. This particularly affects the kidneys which, as a result of a reduced blood flow through them, perform their filtration function less efficiently.
- The tissue walls of the blood vessels, through a loss of elasticity, lose flexibility and become rigid, and are thus less efficient at transporting blood around the body. Blood flow may be further reduced by fatty deposits on the walls of the blood vessels.

The digestive system

The muscles of the alimentary canal, or gut, are used in the following digestive processes:

- moving food along the gut by the process of peristalsis

- keeping the contents of different parts of the alimentary canal separate by areas of thickened muscles called sphincters
- breaking food down into smaller, more manageable, particles
- mixing digestive juices with the food particles.

With the weakening of the gut muscles associated with ageing comes a loss of efficiency in the process of digestion:

- Peristalsis slows down which may cause constipation and other disorders.
- The sphincter muscles become less efficient, so food may enter different sections of the alimentary canal and cause indigestion or other problems.
- Food particles will not be broken down as effectively into small pieces. Consequently, fewer valuable nutrients will be absorbed as the digestive juices can't work as efficiently on larger food particles.

The respiratory system

The amount of air taken into the lungs with each breath reduces with age as a result of a combination of the following factors:

- The muscles of the diaphragm and ribs used in inhalation become weaker and less efficient
- The walls of the alveoli become less elastic so are therefore less able to stretch to take in air
- The alveolar walls thicken, which makes gaseous exchange less efficient
- There are various health disorders which may affect the ability to inhale effectively.

More effort and, therefore, energy are needed in an attempt to take enough air into the lungs. This causes breathlessness and can put extra strain on the heart.

The endocrine system

Thyroxine from the thyroid gland regulates many of the body's metabolic functions. In the ageing person, less thyroxine is produced which causes the metabolic rate to slow down, resulting in less energy and stamina.

Temperature control is also partly regulated by thyroxine, which may account for an increasing inability to cope with temperature changes in old age.

The reproductive system

There are certain physical changes in the male and female reproductive systems that are associated with ageing. However, these changes do not prevent the elderly from wanting or achieving satisfactory sex lives.

The menopause signifies the end of a woman's ability to have babies. Because she no longer ovulates, the hormone levels of progesterone and oestrogen drop, resulting in the following changes:

- the ovaries, uterus and cervix shrink
- the Fallopian tubes shorten
- the muscular walls of the vagina become less elastic
- mucous production diminishes and becomes alkaline.

For men, although they can still father babies, the following reproductive changes occur:

- sperm production diminishes;
- sexual arousal takes longer;
- erections are less frequent, less firm and don't last as long;
- ejaculations are less powerful and less frequent.

These are natural changes not diseases and can be accommodated by the elderly couple as the onset is gradual. The important thing to remember about sexuality is that it is an expression of the need to give and receive affection, and is very easily affected by psychological factors.

Psychological changes

Personality

People do not change character as they age; personality traits that were apparent in youth will still remain in old age, although some traits may diminish and some may become more pronounced.

There are many conflicting theories in books, papers and magazines about ageing and personality. Some say that the emotions are still there but they are not so easily shown, whereas others talk of an increase in emotional reactions. Which viewpoint is right? There is a risk, when making generalisations about such issues, that individuality will be lost. People caring for the elderly need to be constantly aware of the need to respect the old person's individuality, so perpetuating stereotypes about their emotions may do more harm than good. It is probably safe to assume that someone who was emotional in their youth will continue to be emotional in old age and someone who didn't show emotion in youth will continue to hide it in old age.

It is claimed that the elderly become more alienated and introverted from society as they adapt to the prospect of the end of life. Perhaps we should ask whether such behaviour, if it exists, is a reaction to society's attitudes towards the elderly rather than a symptom of ageing.

Intelligence

Equally questionable is the claim made in many publications that intelligence diminishes with old age. It is true that brain cells die off at an increasing rate as we grow older, but evidence has long shown that this does not necessarily mean intelligence reduces commensurately. The majority of the tests used to measure the intelligence levels of the elderly are suspect as they were intended for use with children and young people: results of specifically devised tests suggest that some areas of intelligence may actually increase with age. There is, however, a general consensus that intelligence can remain fairly constant if the person lives a stimulating life. Most people, whatever their age, would score poorly on an intelligence test if their surroundings did not motivate them to learn.

The implications of physical and mental changes

In an ageist society such as ours where youth is worshipped it is easy to justify issues such as compulsory retirement and age limits on jobs by quoting some familiar myths about old age. Many of the physical and mental effects of ageing have far more minor implications than is generally allowed. The elderly are not necessarily stubborn any more than they are forgetful, unable to learn new things, unwilling to adapt or easily upset by crises. We recognise that it is simpler to judge people using stereotypes than it is to take the effort to find out what they are really capable of. So it is important that society is aware of the true needs of the elderly, not just the needs society thinks they ought to have.

For the individual elderly person experiencing these physical and social changes in their life it is particularly important to maintain self-respect. They can be helped to maintain a positive image of themselves by being prepared for old age and encouraged to continue to learn. Some examples of this are:

- Preparation for retirement courses – provided either by community education, self-help and other voluntary groups or the workplace.
- An awareness of the need for financial security through pensions, life assurance etc. well before retirement age.
- Preventive health care – although availability may be dependent upon finances and geography.
- Awareness of the importance of a healthy lifestyle, i.e. a balanced diet, exercise, mental stimulation – many area health authorities are now showing a commitment to improving the lifestyles of their patients of all ages by providing free advice (well-person clinics), fitness education classes, and clubs for the over 60s.

These are just some of the ways to help promote self-respect. There is also the need to feel part of a social group, whether it be a group of friends and like-minded people, or simply the family; most of us want to be needed. People who care for the elderly must bear this in mind at all times and be careful not to treat the elderly individual as if they are an item on the day's task sheet.

Society as a whole, and the decision-makers in particular, need to take heed of the needs of the elderly. Statistically, the proportion of elderly people in society is increasing at quite a rate, so their needs will take on a higher profile. Present-day provision is already inadequate, so there is a pressing urgency for some action to be taken by central and local government, the Health and Social Services and other interested parties. Perhaps the time has come to include the elderly themselves in any planning as they are, after all, the ones who know best what they want.

Key issues – a summary

- Old age is not necessarily a chronological benchmark; in many cases age limits are made for administrative expediency.

- Ageing is thought to be a combination of a number of different factors. Although it is not completely understood, the certainty is that it is something that happens to all of us.

- Deteriorating senses are a cause of many of the accidents involving the elderly.

- The muscles in the body become less efficient which affects the functions of the cardiovascular, digestive and respiratory systems.

- Although the reproductive system undergoes changes, it is not necessary to stop having a fulfilling sex life.

- There is conflicting information about the extent of personality changes in old age. Perhaps we should start to question certain assumptions about the elderly.

- There is an increasing awareness of the benefits of preparing for old age.

- It is vital that we all recognise the need for self-respect amongst the elderly; it can be all too easy to lose this in a task-orientated care situation.

Assignment 3 Changes brought about by ageing and their implications

TASK 1:
THEORIES OF
AGEING

Look at the seven biological theories of ageing and as a group share your opinions on each of them. You can find out more detail about each of the theories, and see if you can find any other theories not covered in this section.

TASK 2:
VISIBLE SIGNS OF
AGEING

There are certain visible signs, such as grey hair, wrinkles, changes in posture and fat distribution etc., that we all associate with ageing. Try to obtain between five and ten photographs representing a range of ages, say from 60 years upwards. Ask friends, colleagues and family to guess the ages of the people in the photographs, and check their accuracy.

When you have done this, check:

- what information they based their guesses on
- what age/sex group tended to be more accurate
- whether they were taken in by stereotypes of ageing, e.g. grey hair, wrinkles, sex of person, etc.

TASK 3: **EYESIGHT**	Longsightedness makes it difficult to focus on close objects. Make some suggestions that would help to reduce the problem.
TASK 4: **HEARING**	Shouting to an elderly person who has high-frequency deafness is no help at all. Find out the best way of helping them to hear what is being said.

TASK 5:
POTENTIAL
DANGERS

List the potential dangers resulting from:

- a deterioration of the sense of balance
- a raised pain threshold
- a wasting of the muscles
- weakening bones
- failing eyesight and hearing
- a less efficient sense of smell and taste.

TASK 6:
CARDIOVASCULAR
SYSTEM

Find a diagram of the cardiovascular system and check that you understand how the blood circulates around the body.

TASK 7:
DIGESTIVE SYSTEM

Check that you understand the following about the digestive system:

- the structure of the alimentary canal (gut)
- the action of peristalsis
- the function of the sphincter muscles
- the way food is broken down.

TASK 8:
RESPIRATORY
SYSTEM

Check that you understand the following about the respiratory system:

- the structure of the respiratory system
- the function of the rib and diaphragm muscles
- how gaseous exchange takes place
- how the lungs are kept clean.

TASK 9:
THYROXINE

Find out about the role of the hormone thyroxine in the body. Include in your research the role of the pituitary gland in the production of thyroxine.

TASK 10:
MENOPAUSE

The onset of the menopause signifies a change in a woman's life as she is no longer able to have children. It is therefore not simply a physical change, there may also be some psychological effects.

(a) Research into the causes, signs and possible symptoms of the menopause, plus any treatments that are available. You may wish to incorporate some of the following suggestions:

- the physical causes
- the physical signs

- possible health problems
- possible psychological and/or emotional effects
- a comparison of theories, i.e. whether ideas have changed over the years. Older theories can often be found in books and papers; more up-to-date research can be found in listings in the British Humanities Index.
- hormone replacement therapy.

(b) More recently, Germaine Greer has attempted to write in a more positive way about the menopause. Look at what she has to say and evaluate her comments in the light of what you have found out from other sources.

TASK 11:
MALE MENOPAUSE

Although men do not have an obvious sign of their changing sexuality, certain changes do occur. Investigate people's attitudes towards the 'male menopause'. You may wish to write a series of questions for people to answer. These questions could cover such issues as:

- whether people believe men have an equivalent to the menopause
- whether people see old age as affecting a man's sexuality
- how much is known about the way ageing affects a man's sexual performance
- the psychological effects a 'male menopause' may have on a man.

TASK 12:
PSYCHOLOGICAL
CHANGES

Find out about research on the changes in personality and intelligence in old age. For each piece of research, briefly outline:

- the date it was carried out
- the conclusions reached.

As a group, evaluate each piece of research and question its implications for the way the elderly are treated.

TASK 13:
CARERS'
GUIDELINES

In the light of what you have found out, your work experience with the elderly and your personal experience of ageing members of the family, prepare a set of guidelines for a carer to follow that will help promote the elderly person's self-respect.

4 Mental health disorders associated with ageing

The number of elderly people suffering from some form of mental health disorder is increasing rapidly as more people are living into their eighties and nineties than ever before.

This creates problems for those in the caring professions who are then faced with decisions on how to maximise the use of a less-than-adequate Health and Social Services provision. For family and friends, however, the effects may be far-reaching and catastrophic. Additional domiciliary help and support from the caring services is vital, as is early diagnosis to prevent the problems from worsening.

As mental health disorders in the elderly are usually coupled with medical or social problems, it is important that there is close liaison between the Health and Social Services personnel so that help and support can be provided as early as possible to prevent the need for residential care for as long as possible.

Stress and anxiety

Signs and causes   To judge from many health reports in the media, stress would seem to be the root cause of most health problems in our everyday lives. However, it is only excessive, uncontrolled stress which is harmful. In order to remain alert and motivated we all need a degree of stress and the elderly are no different in this respect. Stress only becomes a health hazard when we can no longer cope with demands placed upon us and adrenalin builds up and is not dissipated.

Anxiety is one of the more common symptoms of stress and can manifest itself in any of the following ways:

- headaches and migraines
- digestive disorders
- panic attacks
- dizziness and palpitations.

These symptoms can get worse and develop into other, more serious, diseases such as:

- high blood pressure (hypertension)
- heart disease
- peptic ulcers.

Treatment
The fears and anxieties need to be discussed with a professional person who will probably recommend relaxation techniques in the first instance. Clearly, there would be greater success if the cause of the anxiety could be removed, but this is not always possible.

Relaxation techniques may include:

- appropriate exercise (depending on medical advice)
- yoga
- meditation
- counselling
- hypnotherapy.

If these treatments don't work, then the doctor will probably prescribe a mild tranquilliser to suppress the immediate symptoms. However, it is still necessary to find the underlying cause of the problem, otherwise the symptoms will return as soon as the tranquillisers are stopped.

There is also a danger in having too little stress in life. Retirement can lead to feelings of boredom and uselessness, and many of the elderly we see in some of the old-style residential homes are under-stimulated, and this lack of stress in their lives causes them to shut off from everyday life. It is important to try and keep a balance between healthy and stimulating stress levels and no stimulus at all.

Depression

Signs and causes
Anxiety may also be one of the symptoms of depression. Depressive illnesses are quite common in the elderly as they often result from a physical disease, yet they frequently pass undetected as we almost tend to expect the elderly to be less happy and animated.

Depression can be short-term, often in response to a crisis such as illness or bereavement, both of which are likely to be experienced in old age. In this case, depression is a safety mechanism which gives the mind time to adapt to the major changes which are taking place. If the grieving process is not completed (*see* p 152), then depression may set in.

Long-term depression, which may develop if the individual cannot cope with short-term depression, tends to drag the person down, everyday life is an effort and there may even be a loss of the will to live.

A person suffering from depression can exhibit one or more of the following symptoms:

- anxiety and tension
- loss of appetite
- digestive problems
- sleeplessness
- feelings of despair
- apathy and fatigue
- loss of concentration
- suppressed or uncontrolled emotions
- obsessiveness
- irrational fear
- introversion
- feelings of guilt
- slowing down of speech and movements
- loss of interest in sex
- possible suicidal tendencies.

Treatment The doctor first needs to check that there is no underlying physical cause of the depression such as:

- alcoholism
- the onset of dementia
- thyrotoxicosis
- a reaction to prescribed drugs
- infections such as influenza, infectious hepatitis or chest infections.

It is thought that a great many cases of depression remain undiagnosed. Some possible reasons for this are:

- the symptoms may not be acute, so pass unnoticed
- the person doesn't seek help because the nature of the illness makes them withdrawn and apathetic
- people may expect the elderly to be depressed.

There are four main ways of treating depression:

1 By the use of **anti-depressant drugs**. These fall into three main categories:

- the tricyclic drugs, which have few side effects and are more commonly prescribed. They take two to three weeks to take effect and a single dose is usually taken at bedtime to avoid drowsiness the next day. Side effects may be a dry mouth, blurred vision, constipation and drowsiness.
- the monoamine oxidase inhibitors, which are not as frequently prescribed as they can have serious side effects. High blood pressure

may result if the drug is taken in conjunction with certain foods or alcohol. Liver damage may also occur.

- Lithium, taken as a salt called lithium carbonate, works by controlling mood swings. It has to be taken for a long period of time, so the person needs to be monitored for possible problems.

2 **Electroconvulsive therapy (ECT)** is the controlled application of an electrical current to the brain in conjunction with muscle relaxants. As the patient is under a mild anaesthetic, the procedure is painless.

3 **Therapy treatments**, which are a type of discussion between the depressed person, or group of people, and a trained therapist. The main aim is to help the person understand their problems by exploring feelings and discussing them. Here are some of the main types of therapy:

- Counselling, where the person sits and talks about their problems to a counsellor. The counsellor will help them to work out their own solutions to the problem rather than offer advice.
- Individual interpretive and supportive psychotherapy aims to promote the person's understanding of the underlying causes of their problems through various techniques. A psychotherapist will be more specialised than a counsellor.
- Group psychotherapy and psychodrama have the same aims, but work by sharing the experiences with others.

4 If the elderly person needs continued domiciliary support, the following services are available:

- psychiatric community nursing
- day centres
- short and long stay in hospital
- voluntary provision such as meals-on-wheels
- support services such as home help, laundry services
- financial support.

Confusional states

Signs and causes There are many causes of confusional conditions in the elderly. The term is usually applied when a previously confident and competent person becomes completely disorientated in time, place and events.

When the condition has a sudden onset and lasts for anything up to a few months, then it is called acute confusion, or acute brain failure. If it lasts longer, and maybe becomes worse, the condition is described as chronic confusion, or chronic brain failure. Here are some of the symptoms of acute confusion:

- agitation and restlessness
- hallucinations and delusions

- disorientation
- mood changes
- occasional aggression.

Often the disorder is a result of a physical disease, so may well be accompanied by other symptoms such as:

- incontinence
- drowsiness
- fever
- weakness
- feelings of being unwell
- loss of appetite.

Some diseases that may result in acute confusion are:

- infections of the urinary tract, chest or skin
- heart attack
- stroke
- diarrhoea and/or vomiting
- sugar diabetes
- drugs, both those prescribed by the doctor, e.g. treatment for Parkinson's disease, steroids etc., and those bought over the counter.

Acute confusion can also be caused by traumas such as:

- shock as a result of a fall
- upset caused by bereavement
- upheaval, e.g. moving home, hospitalisation etc.

For many elderly people the disorder will not be as dramatic as this; they will feel unwell and will just appear to be acting a little differently from normal.

Treatment   The first step is that someone needs to recognise that there is something wrong and seek medical advice. Once the GP makes a diagnosis, treatment can begin.

Treatment may need to operate on several levels. If the acute confusion is caused by an infection, then antibiotics will be given as treatment, but the person also needs to be kept in a calm and soothing environment and given a suitable diet. If the person is agitated, and drug treatments have not yet taken effect, then they may need to be given tranquillising drugs to calm them down.

Chronic confusion

If the state of confusion lasts for longer than three months, it is called chronic confusion or chronic brain failure. The signs and symptoms of this chronic confusional state can be one or more of the following:

- depression and anxiety
- memory loss
- disorientation
- an inability to cope with everyday life.

Chronic confusional states can be divided into two types of condition:

- treatable conditions which need to be recognised and responded to with appropriate medical care as soon as possible;
- untreatable conditions, known as dementia, for which there are no cures. However, the patient's symptoms may be helped by drug and therapy treatments.

Treatable causes of chronic confusion

- **Metabolic disorders** such as hypothyroidism which is caused by a malfunctioning of the thyroid gland. This condition has a gradual onset so may pass undetected at first. The symptoms are a slowing down of all bodily functions so the sufferer often becomes constipated and puts on weight. The patient finds it difficult to keep warm, the pulse slows down, the voice deepens, and hair is lost from the head and eyebrows. If the disease remains undetected, the mental functions also slow down, leading to a state of chronic confusion. The treatment for this condition is to gradually administer thyroxine so that the body has time to adapt to the metabolic changes.
- **Parkinson's disease** (*see* Chapter 5) affects the nervous system and, in its later stages can lead to confusion. Indeed, in the final stages of the disease there are similarities with Alzheimer's disease (*see* p 36).
- **Alcohol** can be the cause of chronic confusional states either by its overuse or by its sudden withdrawal. Alcohol abuse can cause Korsakoff's psychosis which is a loss of recent memory. However, the sudden withdrawal of alcohol can cause delirium tremens (DTs) – a physical craving for alcohol which is so strong that the sufferer becomes confused and may hallucinate.
- **Head injuries** can cause internal bleeding which causes pressure to build up on the brain. Obviously serious head injuires where bleeding (especially if external) is severe need to be reported to a doctor immediately. Less serious or undetected internal bleeding, however, may pass unnoticed until the onset of symptoms such as confusion and drowsiness. The treatment is to drain off the blood and relieve the pressure. The degree of recovery, however, will be determined by the level of brain damage caused by the incident.
- A **brain tumour** also causes pressure to build up on the brain, resulting in symptoms which include chronic confusion. Most brain tumours in the elderly, however, are malignant and the response to treatments such as radiotherapy or steroids is limited. Non-malignant, or benign,

tumours are more rare and, if discovered, are surgically removed. As the resources involved in investigative techniques are scarce and the costs are high, it is rare for tumours to be diagnosed in the elderly.

- **Untreated syphilis** will, in its final stages, cause chronic confusion along with other mental disorders. Although the condition can still be treated with penicillin, if it has been present for some years a full recovery is unlikely.
- **A deficiency of vitamin B**, which is important for the healthy functioning of the nervous system, can result in tiredness amounting to lethargy and confusion. The condition can be helped by the administration of regular injections of vitamin B.

Although not all these disorders can be treated with 100 per cent success, many of the symptoms can be alleviated or cured by appropriate drug treatments, surgery or therapy. This reinforces the need for speedy and accurate diagnosis, to minimise distress and suffering for all concerned. Unfortunately, all too often the elderly person and their family and/or carer assume that the symptoms are an expected – almost acceptable – part of ageing. This should not be so.

Untreatable chronic confusion – dementia

There are two main types of dementia:

- the Alzheimer type, which accounts for 50 per cent of cases of dementia, and
- multi-infarct disease which accounts for around 20 per cent of cases.

Of the remaining causes, 20 per cent seem to be a mixture of Alzheimer's and multi-infarct disease, with 10 per cent being other dementias.

The signs and symptoms of dementia are:

- gradual onset of the symptoms, with the person retaining awareness for a time
- loss of concentration
- memory loss, especially short-term memory in the first stages and long-term in the later stages
- disorientation of time, place and events, especially when out of familiar surroundings
- reduced ability to learn new things
- behavioural changes, e.g. becoming noisy, aggressive, dirty, losing social inhibitions etc.
- wandering
- incontinence, more often urinary than faecal, which can be voluntary or involuntary (*see* p 141)
- problems with dressing and feeding
- difficulty in communicating
- disturbed sleep patterns
- emotional changes
- apathy.

There is little treatment for dementia, and certainly no cure. Restlessness and aggression can be controlled by drugs, but the major responsibility lies with the family and/or carer who need all the help and support they can get.

Assessment will be carried out by a process of liaison between any of the following professionals:

- initial referral to GP
- psychiatrist
- geriatrician
- psychogeriatrician
- neurologist
- clinical psychologist.

Alzheimer's disease

Alzheimer's disease is caused by the grey matter in the brain, the cerebral cortex, undergoing certain changes. The nerve endings in the cortex thicken and tangles occur within the brain cells, or neurons. The more obvious the changes, the more severe the dementia.

Those with an increased risk of developing Alzheimer's disease are people with:

- a family history of the disease
- a family history of thyroid disease
- a family history of Down's syndrome
- a previous head injury.

Research is being carried out to find ways of helping sufferers of Alzheimer's disease. Areas of research are:

- the causes, i.e. whether it is genetic, viral, as a result of toxins or a chemical imbalance
- methods of early detection
- the care of sufferers
- the needs of the family and/or carers.

Multi-infarct dementia

Multi-infarct dementia occurs when areas of the brain are destroyed by a series of small strokes. The strokes cut off the blood supply to part of the brain which then becomes permanently damaged. The damage may only be enough to cause memory loss, or it can lead to weakness in the limbs and difficulty with speech.

The main cause of these strokes is a furring up of the arteries leading to the brain – **atheroma** – and affects men more than women. Deterioration can take almost regular steps as more strokes occur.

Those with an increased risk of developing multi-infarct disease include people who:

- have a heart disorder
- suffer from high blood pressure (hypertension)
- have a family history of heart disease
- are male
- have a higher risk of heart and circulatory diseases through, e.g. smoking, drinking, being overweight, etc.
- are diabetic.

People in these at-risk groups, or those who have suffered from strokes, should try to change to a healthier lifestyle to help reduce blood pressure.

Other forms of dementia

The other, lesser known, forms of dementia are:

- **Binswanger's disease**, where the white matter rather than the grey matter of the brain is affected. The symptoms may be erratic, with periods of remission.
- **Creutzfeldt-Jakob disease**, which is exceptionally rare and thought to be caused by a virus.
- **Pick's disease**, with symptoms similar to Alzheimer's disease, is caused by enlarged and abnormal neurons. It is more likely to affect the young elderly, and death follows within a few years.

The implications of dementia

The implications for the family and/or carer are immense. Dementia has been called a 'living death' as the personality of the sufferer has died, leaving only their body behind, inhabited by a stranger.

Initially, after diagnosis, the sufferer will probably live in the home with their spouse or another relative as the carer and with support from the caring services. The carer's needs, however, must not be ignored as their lives will be very difficult, depending on the level of the sufferer's disability. The carer will feel, at varying times, grief, anger, resentment, alienation, shame and general exhaustion. It is important for the carer to make use of all the help and support that can be offered by the caring services. This, however, is rarely adequate, especially since cut-backs in funding have coincided with significant increases in demand.

Eventually it becomes necessary for the sufferer to be admitted into residential care or hospital, once their condition has deteriorated to such an extent that they become a danger to themselves and/or others. The carer may well feel guilty and inadequate at this stage, but the decision will have been based on medical evidence. Staff at the residential centre or hospital need to be aware of the feelings of the carer, and should try to keep them informed and involved.

Key issues – a summary

- As we grow older we are more likely to suffer from some sort of mental health disorder.

- Nowadays there are more eighty and ninety-year-olds than ever before, so there are increasing numbers of people with mental health disorders needing care and support from an apparently diminishing public care sector purse. This inevitably puts additional strain on the immediate family and friends of the sufferer.

- The various professional personnel dealing with the mentally disordered person will need to liaise closely in order to ensure all their client's needs are dealt with.

- Positive stress is good for the elderly as it motivates them and keeps them involved in everyday life. Without any form of stress, a person can become apathetic and depressed. People caring for the elderly need to be aware of this.

- Stress of the wrong type has a negative effect and can cause physical symptoms.

- Treatment of stress and anxiety may take the form of changing to a healthier lifestyle coupled with counselling and/or drug treatment.

- Depression first needs to be recognised, which is not always straightforward, then the cause needs to be found, i.e. whether it is the result of a physical or mental illness.

- Depression needs to be treated as quickly as possible as it has a very detrimental effect on the quality of life. It is never right to expect depression just because of age; there is always an underlying cause.

- The term 'acute confusion' is used if the condition lasts for less than three months.

- Early diagnosis is important as acute confusion can be a symptom of a physical disorder.

- Chronic confusion is when the symptoms last for more than three months. For some of the cases, the symptoms can be either alleviated or cured, so early diagnosis is important.

- Untreatable confusional states fall into two main categories: the Alzheimer types and the multi-infarct types. Some of the symptoms can be helped by drug and therapy treatments, but there is no cure. The carer and families need a great deal of support at this time to help them cope with the disorder which has been called a living death.

■ The majority of the elderly suffering from confusional states are cared for at home, usually by a member of their family. The most pressing problem for the carers is the feeling of being alone with very little support, and little recognition of their own needs. The over-stretched caring services will offer some support, but often the greatest help will come from family, friends, voluntary self-help groups and, possibly, the Church.

The number of elderly suffering from confusional states is increasing along with life expectancy, yet the caring services are already working to capacity, and there are, as yet, no plans for change. The implications are, therefore, that the brunt of care provision will fall on the carer at home, the majority of whom are women.

Assignment 4 Ageing and mental health disorders

TASK 1:
STRESS AND THE
ELDERLY

The elderly are just as likely to suffer from the symptoms of stress as the rest of society. In order to understand the problems stress may cause, you will need to find out the following information:

- the function of adrenalin in the body
- a definition of stress
- examples of stressful situations in an elderly person's life
- the short-term effects of stress on the body and mind
- the long-term effects of stress on the body and mind.

When you have collected this information, as a group consider these areas in relation to the elderly:

- the way short- and long-term stress could affect their everyday lives
- warning signs that the carer and/or the family should look for
- various ways of treating and/or preventing stress, including drug treatments, relaxation techniques, and counselling.

TASK 2:
AVOIDING UNDER-
STIMULATION

As a group, discuss ways that day centres and residential homes for the elderly can avoid the problem of too little stimulus in the day-to-day lives of their clients.

TASK 3:
DEPRESSION

Depression can be short or long-term and can be triggered off by any number of circumstances. In the elderly, however, depression often remains undiagnosed.

As a group discuss:

(*a*) why you think it remains undiagnosed;
(*b*) steps the caring services can take to improve on pick-up rates.

TASK 4:
DEPRESSION, ITS
PHYSICAL CAUSES
	Depression may have an underlying physical cause; some of these are listed on p 31. To make sure that you understand how physical conditions can lead to feelings of depression, carry out the following research:
	(a) alcoholism
	    ● how an elderly person could become dependent on alcohol
	    ● the effects of alcohol on the body
	    ● the effects of alcohol on the mind
	    ● the symptoms of alcoholism.
	(b) thyrotoxicosis
	    ● the functions of the thyroid gland
	    ● the function of thyroxine
	    ● the effects of over- and under-activity of the gland
	    ● the symptoms of thyrotoxicosis.
	(c) illness (influenza, infectious hepatitis, chest infection)
	    ● the symptoms of each
	    ● how they affect the body in such a way as to cause depression.

TASK 4:

DEPRESSION, ITS

PHYSICAL CAUSES

Depression may have an underlying physical cause; some of these are listed on p 31. To make sure that you understand how physical conditions can lead to feelings of depression, carry out the following research:

(a) alcoholism
- how an elderly person could become dependent on alcohol
- the effects of alcohol on the body
- the effects of alcohol on the mind
- the symptoms of alcoholism.

(b) thyrotoxicosis
- the functions of the thyroid gland
- the function of thyroxine
- the effects of over- and under-activity of the gland
- the symptoms of thyrotoxicosis.

(c) illness (influenza, infectious hepatitis, chest infection)
- the symptoms of each
- how they affect the body in such a way as to cause depression.

TASK 5:

ANTI-DEPRESSANT

DRUGS

The following drugs may be prescribed to help relieve depression:
- the tricyclic drugs
- the monoamine oxidase inhibitors
- lithium.

Look them up in a drugs listing book and find out:
- their trade names
- how long they need to be taken
- when they are likely to be prescribed
- any contraindications.

TASK 6:

ECT

Find out more about Electroconvulsive Therapy (ECT). As well as finding out how the process is carried out, also look at:

- its history
- the type of person who would be given the treatment
- its advantages and disadvantages.

TASK 7:

THERAPIES FOR

DEPRESSION

Research into the types of therapies available to the depressed elderly in your area. Include:

- counselling
- psychotherapy
- group psychotherapy and psychodrama.

Look at whether the service is free of charge, subsidised or charged for, and whether it is easily available.

TASK 8:

STATES OF

CONFUSION

There is a mass of confusional conditions, some are temporary, others are permanent; some are treatable, others can only be partly controlled.

To help you to understand what at first appears to be a confusing wealth of signs, symptoms, causes and treatments, compile an at-a-glance table. The following ideas may help:

- the differences between the terms, acute and chronic confusion
- the symptoms of acute confusion
- possible causes of acute confusion, split into:
  —diseases
  —traumas
- the treatment(s)
- the symptoms of treatable chronic confusion
- possible causes of treatable chronic confusion, split into:
  —metabolic disorders
  —diseases
  —alcoholism
  —trauma or tumour to brain
  —deficiency
- treatment(s)
- the symptoms of untreatable chronic confusion
- the four main causes of untreatable chronic confusion
- possible ways of managing the condition.

TASK 9: ALZHEIMER'S DISEASE AND THE CARERS

Alzheimer's disease has been called a 'living death'. Look at the effects the disease could have on the carer and/or family of the sufferer. Information can be found by:

- library research, looking at books, articles (listed in the British Humanities Index) and research papers;
- contacting local caring services;
- contacting local voluntary agencies (information can be found at Citizens Advice Bureaux, libraries, doctors' surgeries, etc.);
- from the Alzheimer's Disease Society, 158/160 Balham High Road, London SW12 9BN.

TASK 10: SUGGESTIONS FOR IMPROVED PROVISION

When you have completed the tasks above, you will have become aware of the many problems facing the family and/or carer of someone suffering from a confusional disorder. Compile a set of suggestions that you think should be implemented by:

- central and local government;
- voluntary and statutory agencies;
- the National Health Service; and
- Social Services

in order to cope with the ever-increasing demands for mental health provision for the elderly.

5 Physical disorders associated with ageing

As the body ages it is almost inevitable that some form of health disorder will eventually develop, even if it is a relatively minor one. Occasionally, however, the disorder may be serious.

This chapter will look at symptoms, causes and possible treatments of various physical disorders that may develop in old age. It must be remembered, however, that, though the incidence of these diseases increases with age, many of these health disorders can affect anyone in the population and are not solely associated with the elderly. Indeed, many health disorders which are diagnosed in old age start in middle age – or even earlier.

Patterns of ill-health

In old age, diseases are diagnosed that may have started earlier in life. For example, a person who has smoked may develop lung cancer, one who has eaten a diet high in fats may suffer a stroke, and degenerative diseases such as arthritis will become worse and affect movement. These types of diseases, some of which are likely to become the ultimate causes of death, may be brought about by:

- the process of ageing
- environmental dangers such as pollution or asbestos
- heredity
- a poor living environment, e.g. poverty
- a poor diet, e.g. malnutrition; too much fat, sugar or salt; too little fibre, etc.
- smoking
- alcohol abuse
- drug abuse, either of prescribed or non-prescribed drugs
- lack of exercise.

Alternatively, the disease may be the result of an infection or an accident.

Diagnosis and treatment

Health disorders in the elderly are often more difficult to diagnose than those of a younger person because of the following factors:

- The elderly are less likely to present their symptoms to a doctor, often because they think the symptoms are all part of growing old.
- Disorders that would cause a great deal of pain in a younger person, such as a heart attack or appendicitis, may cause little more than discomfort to the elderly person. This is probably due to the raising of the pain threshold (*see* Chapter 3).
- There may be more than one disorder giving rise to the symptoms.
- The elderly person, if confused, may be less able to describe symptoms accurately when they do see a doctor.

As with any disease affecting any age group, the quicker the disease is diagnosed, the earlier possible treatment can be started. However, diagnosis of disease in the elderly is even more important since, because their powers of recuperation are reduced, disease is relatively more dangerous.

Very few elderly people want to be dependent on others so early treatment offers them the hope of a return to health. However, should the disease ultimately lead to dependency, the carer or the sufferer's family must remember to treat their patient with dignity and respect, and maintain mental stimulation.

Disorders affecting mobility

Arthritis

There are two basic types of arthritis – **osteoarthritis** and **rheumatoid arthritis** – though **gout** is also considered to be an arthritic condition.

Osteoarthritis

By the time they reach old age most people will have some signs of osteoarthritis as a result of general wear and tear on the joints. Overuse or trauma to the joints in earlier life will increase the likelihood of developing the condition (*see* Fig 5.1).

The condition is caused by the wearing down of the layer of cartilage covering the bones at a joint (*see* Fig 5.2). As this smooth covering is worn away, friction within the joint increases, causing creaking, grinding and, eventually, pain. With the onset of pain, the sufferer tends to use the joints less and this weakens the surrounding muscles, making them less able to support the joint. In time, small areas of bone build up around the arthritic joints, becoming visible as nodules on the affected joint.

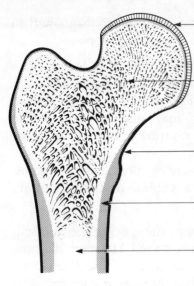

Cartilage covers the ends of the bone at the positions of the joints. It is also present in the growth regions of young bones.

Spongy bone gets its name because of the numerous small spaces within it and not because it is soft and sponge-like. It is neither as strong nor as heavy as compact bone because the spaces are filled with fat or marrow. The blood within spongy bone gives it a pinkish colour. Spongy bone is strengthened by a criss-cross network of **bony supports**. They form in places where extra strength is needed and follow the lines of stress.

Periosteum (peri = around; osteum = bone) covers the remainder of the bone that is not covered by cartilage. This thin, tough membrane is firmly attached to the bone and is almost impossible to remove. There is a network of **nerves** in the periosteum.

Compact bone forms an outer layer and is thickest in those places which receive the greatest stress. Its dense texture gives it strength but makes it heavy.

Central cavity is present only in long bones (those which have an elongated shape) and is filled with marrow or fat. There can be a cavity in the centre of long bone because this region is not required to take any load or other stress. It makes the bone lighter without loss of strength and allows the space to be used for other purposes.

Fig 5.1 Inside a bone

The larger and the more frequently used joints are more likely to be affected:

- hips
- knees
- hands
- ankles
- feet.

There is no cure for osteoarthritis but the symptoms may be relieved by any of the following:

- anti-inflammatory drugs
- pain-killing drugs
- hip replacement
- physiotherapy
- specialised aids and equipment
- exercise and walking
- keeping weight down.

Rheumatoid arthritis

This inflammatory condition is less common than osteoarthritis but it can be more debilitating. It tends to affect the smaller joints such as those in the arms and shoulders, i.e. fingers, hands, wrists, elbows and shoulders. It can also affect the organs of the body such as the heart, the lungs and the eyes. Affecting more women than men, rheumatoid arthritis can start very early in life, even attacking children, though its incidence is far higher in the elderly.

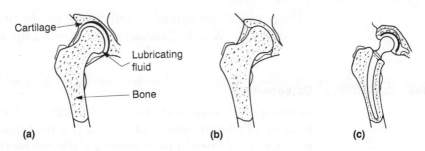

Fig 5.2 Cartilage at the end of bone (a) Normal joint (b) Joint damaged by arthritis (c) Artificial hip in position

The pain is caused by an inflammation of the synovial membrane lining the joints and tendon sheaths. The inflamed membrane may then overgrow the joints and eat into the bone and cartilage.

The symptoms of the disease are:

- general feeling of ill-health and possible weight loss
- painful and stiff joints, usually starting in the hands and feet
- swelling of the finger joints and possible nodules
- more joints become affected, becoming swollen, stiff, hot and painful
- the joints will eventually become deformed, followed by muscle wastage
- anaemia and depression may develop.

The disease varies in severity, with some people being affected only slightly while others are badly disabled. It also varies in its onset; in some cases starting slowly and progressing gradually, while in others it starts suddenly, appearing almost overnight.

Treatment of rheumatoid arthritis is about controlling symptoms since there is, as yet, no cure. One of the main symptoms is joint stiffness and this may be alleviated by exercises devised by physiotherapists which may be done at any time except during the active stages of the disease. The main treatments as the disease worsens are painkilling and anti-inflammatory drugs.

Gout

This condition is caused by a build-up of uric acid crystals in the joint cavity and in the case of acute gout attacks the joint becomes very painful for up to ten days. The skin around the affected area may become red and eventually peel. The pain then goes and the joint returns to normal. In chronic cases the joint may become deformed and the kidneys may also suffer damage. The joint most likely to be affected is the big toe, but the ankles, wrists and fingers may also suffer.

Gout is very often associated, though not solely, with the elderly – the stereotypical sufferer being a heavy-drinking old man. Though the stereotype is perhaps unfair, the disease does affect eight times as many men as women.

Drugs can be prescribed to reduce the production of uric acid in the blood stream. Anti-inflammatory drugs will help an acute gout attack.

Bone disorders

Osteoporosis

In osteoporosis there is a reduction and weakening of the bone mass which leads to a higher incidence of injuries and fractures. The disease is more prevalent in women as their bones are affected by the hormonal changes of the menopause.

One of the first symptoms is a severe or chronic backache, although the disease can eventually cause loss of height and spinal deformities – commonly known as dowager's hump – in elderly women. The main problem is that the elderly suffering from osteoporosis are very likely to fracture bones as a result of relatively small accidents or falls.

Although there is no real treatment, the condition is best prevented by taking vitamin D and calcium supplements in earlier life. For women, hormone replacement therapy (HRT) has proved to be an effective, though controversial, preventive measure. Regular exercise is usually advised by physiotherapists.

Osteomalacia

Osteomalacia is the adult equivalent of rickets and is caused by vitamin D deficiency. The likely causes are:

- a diet deficient in vitamin D
- lack of sunlight
- liver or kidney disorders.

The symptoms are:

- painful bones
- possible bone deformity
- increased likelihood of fractures
- a waddling walk.

Early diagnosis can help prevent fractures. Treatment is usually to give carefully monitored vitamin D supplements.

Paget's disease

Paget's disease is more likely to be found in some countries than others, and is rarely found in Africa, the Far East, Switzerland or Scandinavia. It is caused by an increase in the production and reabsorption of the bone which results in painful, spongy, enlarged and deformed areas of affected bone. The skull, pelvis, tibia, femur, spine and shoulder blade are most frequently affected.

The condition may be complicated by:

- swollen bones pressing on nerves, especially those of the spinal cord
- an increased likelihood of fractures
- a chance that the affected areas could become malignant
- hearing and visual impairment.

Bone pain is treated with pain-killers. More serious cases may be given calcitonin hormone injections, but this is rare as it is very expensive.

Other causes of reduced mobility

- Neurological diseases such as Parkinson's disease (*see* p 78); multiple sclerosis; Alzheimer's disease (*see* p 36).
- Strokes (*see* p 76)
- Circulatory problems, e.g. intermittent claudication which, if the condition degenerates, can cause gangrene resulting in eventual amputation.
- Foot disorders
- Impairment of the sense of balance, known as **kinetic impairment**, may occur if the cerebellum, the part of the brain which governs balance, is damaged in any way. Impairment can result from damage to the brain, tumours or general degeneration.
- Poorly controlled diabetes which can also have complications which result in amputation.

Disorders of the cardio-vascular system

Atherosclerosis This is a major health problem in the western world, accounting for around half of all deaths and causing a great deal of disability for those who survive. It is also the main cause of heart attacks, strokes and other disorders of the blood vessels.

Atherosclerosis is the build-up of fatty deposits, called **atheroma**, on the walls of the blood vessels. These fatty deposits are made up of

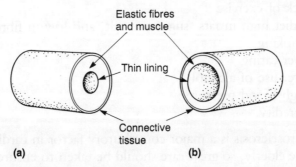

(a) (b)

Fig 5.3 Structure of artery and vein (a) Structure of an artery
(b) Structure of a vein

The pressure of blood pushes
open the valve and allows the
blood to flow through

When the pressure is relaxed,
the valve closes and stops
blood flowing back

Fig 5.4 Section through a vein to show how a valve works

cholesterol and fibrous tissue and adhere to the walls in a patchy fashion
that will eventually cause a partial or complete blockage of the blood flow.
The deposits grow into large areas called plaques, and other harden, causing
a condition known as **sclerosis**.

Up until late middle-age, the disorder is more prevalent in men, after
which age women start to develop the symptoms. The problem may start
in childhood or adolescence as the fatty deposits build up on the blood
vessel walls.

The diseases resulting from a narrowing of the arteries are:

- blood clots, known as thrombosis
- heart diseases such as angina and ischaemic heart disease
- intermittent claudication as a result of reduced blood flow
- sensory disturbances if the brain is affected
- infarction.

The diseases resulting from blocking of the arteries are:

- coronary thrombosis if the heart is affected
- strokes if the brain is affected
- arterial thrombosis.

Although the cause of atherosclerosis is not completely understood, it is
known that there are a number of contributory factors. These include:

- lack of exercise
- a diet high in fats, sugar and salt, and low in fibre
- smoking
- over-eating
- over-use of alcohol
- high blood pressure
- heredity.

Atherosclerosis is a major contributory factor in cardio-vascular diseases
of the elderly, so great care should be taken to ensure a healthy lifestyle
in order to prevent it from developing. Should any symptoms develop,
then a visit to the doctor for diagnosis is essential.

Heart disease   There are four main diseases of the coronary arteries. These are:

- angina pectoris
- heart attacks caused by either a coronary thrombosis or myocardial infarction
- heart failure
- heart block.

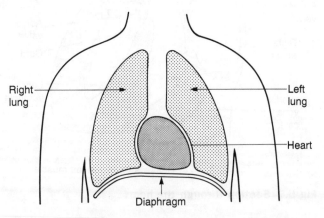

Fig 5.5 Diagram to show the position of the heart

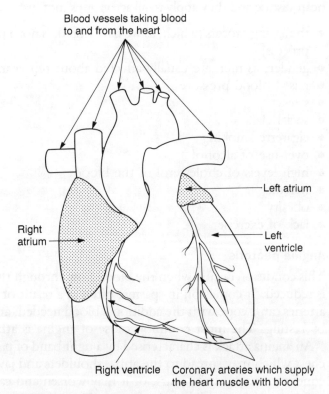

Fig 5.6 The heart from the outside

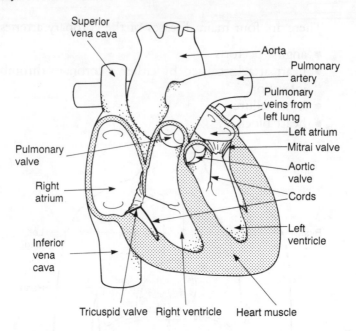

Fig 5.7 Section through the heart

There are certain factors which are known to increase the risk of developing heart disease and they apply to all age groups, not just the elderly. These are:

- the ageing process (which, as we have noted, is not a purely chronological process)
- gender, as men are usually affected about ten years ahead of women
- raised blood pressure
- stress
- social class
- cigarette smoking
- over-use of alcohol
- high levels of cholesterol in the blood
- heredity
- obesity
- lack of exercise.

Angina pectoris

This condition occurs when the blood flow through the coronary arteries is reduced. It comes on in spasms, often as a result of exertion when the arteries can't cope with the additional blood needed, and is usually helped by resting. The most common cause of angina is atherosclerosis.

An angina attack is characterised by a tight band of pain across the upper chest which may spread to the arms, shoulders and jaw (*see* Fig 5.8). The condition may last for years, or it may worsen and cause a heart attack.

Treatment is usually in the form of Trinitrin tablets which are placed

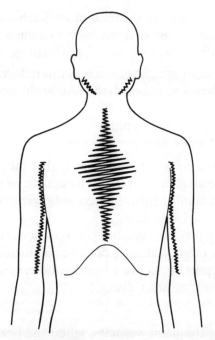

Fig 5.8 Angina pectoris – where the pain is felt

under the tongue, preferably before, but certainly in the early stages of an attack. This drug dilates the blood vessels, so allowing the blood to flow more easily. It can cause a headache. Beta-blockers and other drug treatments may be prescribed for more serious cases.

Heart attacks

Heart attacks are caused by either myocardial infarction or a coronary thrombosis, both of which are usually caused by atherosclerosis. **Myocardial infarction** is when part of the heart muscle has died as a result of blood starvation. **Coronary thrombosis** occurs when the blood supply to the heart muscles is halted by a blood clot.

The symptoms of a heart attack include:

- severe pains in the chest, often spreading down the arms, neck and jaw. The pain comes on suddenly but, unlike angina, it is not necessarily linked with over-exertion and it does not stop when at rest
- fall in blood pressure
- anxiety and cold sweats
- speeding up or slowing down of the heart rate.

Certain symptoms may start well before the attack, but often pass unnoticed. These include:

- tiredness and lethargy
- indigestion
- shortness of breath.

Fast and effective treatment is vital as most deaths occur within the first hour. After this hour the risk of death starts to diminish and approximately 80 per cent of sufferers will recover. Treatment generally includes:

- to prop patient in an upright position as this reduces strain on the heart
- try to induce relaxation, although this is difficult, especially if the sufferer is hospitalised
- pain relief by heroin or morphine
- management of heart-beat irregularities.

In the very elderly or infirm, it is quite likely that they will be left at home if that is where the attack took place. The benefit of this is that they will be more relaxed in familiar surroundings as hospital, with all its specialist equipment, can be very daunting.

After the healing process, which takes weeks or even months, there is no reason why the original lifestyle can't be resumed if the doctor agrees. It is, however, important to live a healthy lifestyle, avoiding the factors that increase the risk of heart disease.

Heart failure

Heart failure is, as the name suggests, when the heart is no longer able to cope with pumping blood around the body. As a result, the blood returning to the heart causes a back-log and pressure is built up. Heart failure can be **acute**, which has a sudden onset, or **congestive**, which has a more gradual build-up.

The causes include:

- high blood pressure
- severe anaemia
- coronary thrombosis
- inflamation of the heart
- smoking
- obesity
- overactive thyroid gland
- ischaemic heart disease, when the blood supply to the heart is restricted.

The symptoms of heart failure are:

- breathlessness as the lungs become flooded by fluid filling the air spaces. The sufferer may have noticed the breathlessness before and often tends to sleep in a propped-up position
- speaking will be difficult
- breathing will sound bubbly
- severe coughing and occasionally bronchitis
- swollen feet and ankles.

The symptoms may last for a few hours or may become chronic.

Treatment of the acute condition will be a diuretic injection so the fluid will be excreted from the body as urine, plus drugs to control high blood pressure and irregular heart beat. Morphine may be given to help relax the patient and relieve the breathlessness.

Congestive heart failure also leads to build-up of fluid. The lungs are still affected, but not so dramatically, and there is a gradual increase in breathlessness. The legs become fluid-filled, a condition known as **oedema**.

Treatment of chronic heart failure is again by diuretic drugs, but they can be taken in tablet form. These drugs need to be carefully monitored as they can have unpleasant side-effects.

Generally, heart failure can be cured if the underlying cause is treatable, such as an underactive thyroid gland, high blood pressure and some heart diseases. In the more serious cases, however, when the heart is under a great deal of strain, the outlook is less favourable.

Heart block

This condition arises when there is a block or partial block in the heart muscle which causes the electrical impulse governing the heart beat to become erratic. The result is that the heart chambers, the **ventricles**, act independently of each other and beat more slowly than usual.

In severe blocks, the sufferer will feel dizzy and may faint or have a fit. In more serious cases the sufferer will have a cardiac arrest, lose consciousness and fall to the ground. In this instance, the sufferer will need to be resuscitated.

Treatment may be the fitting of a pacemaker to regulate the heartbeat.

Other cardio-vascular disorders

- Heartbeat irregularities, known as **arrhythmias**, are usually a symptom of most heart disorders. In the elderly, however, they can simply be caused by fibrosis of the tissues carrying the electrical messages from the brain. Missed or extra beats are not unusual in the elderly.
- High blood pressure, or **hypertension**, is when blood pressure is constantly above the acceptable range. The dangers of undiagnosed hypertension are an increased likelihood of:
  —coronary heart disease
  —heart failure
  —stroke
  —diseases of the arteries.
  With the elderly, however, the treatment often causes unpleasant side-effects, so it is only given if there is reason to believe the benefits outweigh the disadvantages. Hypertension itself isn't the danger, it is the disorders that may result from it.
- Low blood pressure, or **hypotension**, can be:
  —a symptom of accidental or deliberate poisoning
  —a reaction to the drugs used to treat hypertension
  —a result of a malfunction of the body mechanisms controlling blood pressure
  —dehydration.

The symptoms of low blood pressure are dizziness, especially when the sufferer stands up after sitting for some time, and a feeling of shakiness and confusion.

In mild cases, simple exercises can be done or drugs to help retain salt may be prescribed.

- **Intermittent claudication** is a painful condition arising when the blood cannot reach the leg because the main artery to the leg is blocked. The main cause of the blockage is atherosclerosis, but it may be the result of a thrombosis.

  In less severe cases a change in lifestyle may be enough to prevent the condition from worsening. In more severe cases, however, the condition will degenerate to such an extent that the artery will no longer be able to supply enough blood to the leg at rest. The pain is severe and the leg may become ulcerated and then gangrenous.

  Treatment in severe cases is to either remove the affected artery and replace it by grafted tissue or to carry out a by-pass operation. If gangrene has developed, then amputation is necessary.

- **Deep vein and pulmonary thrombosis**. A blood clot may develop in the deep veins of the leg, travel through the bloodstream, and lodge in the pulmonary artery. The condition can be caused by immobility, perhaps as a result of bedrest after an operation for example. Sometimes, however, there is no apparent reason.

  The leg becomes swollen and very painful. The pulmonary embolism will block or partially block the pulmonary artery or its major branches, causing damage or infarction. The symptoms are coughing, breathlessness, fainting and feverishness. A large clot will cause death.

  Anti-coagulant drugs are the usual treatment, but the patient will need to be carefully monitored as such drugs are potentially dangerous, especially when taken in conjunction with other medication.

Disorders of the respiratory system

As the lungs age there is a reduction in their effectiveness which means less oxygen is derived from the air inhaled. This happens gradually and is quite normal, so the body has time to adapt. The normal changes in the lungs associated with ageing are:

- reduction in elasticity of the lung tissue
- reduction in the size of the chest cavity
- loss of efficiency of the respiratory muscles.

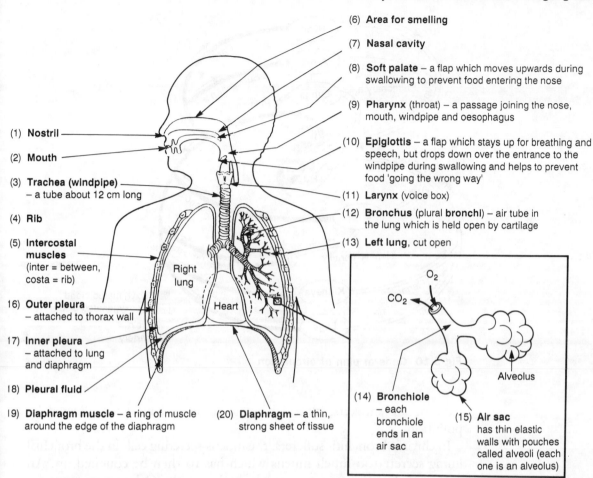

(1) **Nostril**

(2) **Mouth**

(3) **Trachea (windpipe)** – a tube about 12 cm long

(4) **Rib**

(5) **Intercostal muscles** (inter = between, costa = rib)

16) **Outer pleura** – attached to thorax wall

17) **Inner pleura** – attached to lung and diaphragm

18) **Pleural fluid**

19) **Diaphragm muscle** – a ring of muscle around the edge of the diaphragm

(20) **Diaphragm** – a thin, strong sheet of tissue

Right lung

Heart

(6) **Area for smelling**

(7) **Nasal cavity**

(8) **Soft palate** – a flap which moves upwards during swallowing to prevent food entering the nose

(9) **Pharynx** (throat) – a passage joining the nose, mouth, windpipe and oesophagus

(10) **Epiglottis** – a flap which stays up for breathing and speech, but drops down over the entrance to the windpipe during swallowing and helps to prevent food 'going the wrong way'

(11) **Larynx** (voice box)

(12) **Bronchus** (plural **bronchi**) – air tube in the lung which is held open by cartilage

(13) **Left lung**, cut open

O_2

CO_2

Alveolus

(14) **Bronchiole** – each bronchiole ends in an air sac

(15) **Air sac** has thin elastic walls with pouches called alveoli (each one is an alveolus)

Fig 5.9 Respiratory system

The elderly do tend to suffer from more lung diseases for two main reasons:

- their resistance to disease is lowered as their immune system is weakened by ageing
- living and working in a polluted atmosphere or smoking will have taken its toll.

Bronchitis

Bronchitis has two types: acute and chronic.

Acute bronchitis affects the airways. The symptoms are a cough, fever and phlegm which last for 7–10 days. The condition may be the result of a bacterial or viral infection causing inflammation.

The condition needs to be monitored in the elderly as it can lead to pneumonia. Treatment by antibiotics is usually effective.

Chronic bronchitis affects the lining of the bronchi. The term chronic means that it recurs regularly, usually in winter. Over 90 per cent of sufferers

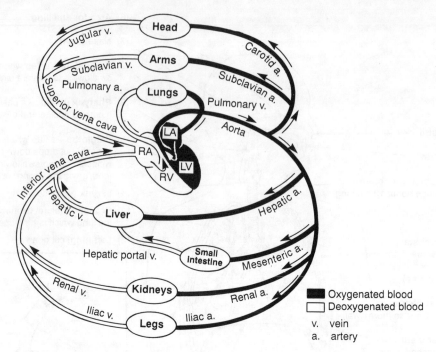

Fig 5.10 General plan of circulation

were or are smokers, although some sufferers have been affected by pollution.

In chronic bronchitis sufferers, the mucus-secreting cells in the bronchial lining secrete too much mucus which has to then be coughed up. An example of this is the typical smoker's cough. Other symptoms are increasingly severe breathlessness, chest pains and a feeling of general ill-health. The sufferer is more likely to develop bouts of acute bronchitis and complications such as emphysema, heart failure or pneumonia may result.

Pneumonia

Pneumonia is a severe inflammation of the lungs caused by either a bacterial or viral infection. The symptoms of the condition are:

- a persistent dry cough
- fever
- chest pain, which may suggest pleurisy
- illness
- rapid breathing
- occasionally confusion.

Pneumonia can be localised in one area of the lung – lobar pneumonia – or spread randomly throughout the lung area – broncho-pneumonia. The condition is quite common in the sick elderly and may result from:

- being bedridden
- heart failure
- bronchitis
- a stroke
- cancer.

Often it is the cause of death in someone who has had a serious illness and has been called 'the old man's friend' as it is relatively painless.

Treatment of bacterial pneumonia is by antibiotics, otherwise the treatment is symptom management.

Pleurisy

Pleurisy is a condition where the pleural surfaces are inflamed. There are two types of pleurisy:

- dry, when the pleural membrane is affected
- wet, when excess fluid is produced.

Pleurisy is often the result of another disease. It may also be caused by pneumonia, an injury to the chest, or cancer. Occasionally there is no apparent cause.

The symptoms for both types are similar and are:

- sharp pain in the chest when breathing
- dry cough
- fever
- diminished breathing sounds
- a dull sound when the chest cavity is tapped.

Treatment is first to check whether there is an underlying cause. In wet pleurisy, the excess fluid may have to be drained off. Painkillers may be needed.

Asthma

Old people with previously healthy lungs can develop asthma. The symptoms of this type of asthma often occur at night and are:

- a tight feeling in the chest
- coughing
- wheezing
- difficulty in breathing out
- raised pulse.

The cause of asthma at this stage could be reaction to an infection or emotional shock.

Treatment is by inhaling drugs that dilate the bronchi or, in more serious cases, the long-term use of corticosteroids may be necessary.

Emphysema

This condition results from a combination of chronic bronchitis and old age. The air sacs in the lungs, the **alveoli**, distend to such an extent that the walls become thin and rupture. One of the main contributory causes is smoking.

The sufferer has the following symptoms:

- breathlessness caused by the loss of elasticity
- effort in breathing
- enlarged chest
- blue lips
- weight loss
- hyperventilation.

Treatment is to see whether the patient has any other conditions that may respond to treatment. The sufferer may need readily-accessible oxygen at home to assist breathing. Once the disease has a hold there is little in the way of treatment. The long-term effects are a strain on the heart which may cause heart failure.

Lung cancer

Lung cancer is a malignant growth which affects one or both lungs. It is the fourth most common cause of death in the UK after heart disease, strokes and pneumonia. The disease is very strongly linked to cigarette smoking, although it can be caused by passive smoking and industrial hazards such as asbestos.

The symptoms are:

- a dry cough
- yellow phlegm
- coughing up blood
- breathlessness after exertion
- loss of appetite and weight loss
- pain in the chest area
- hoarse voice.

The long-term outlook is not good, especially in the elderly. Radiotherapy and chemotherapy may help some cases, but surgery has a low success rate in the elderly. The main help that can be offered is counselling for the sufferer and their family.

Disorders of the digestive system

In old age there is a general increase in the number of digestive disorders experienced by people. Certain of these symptoms may have additional importance as they could be signs of disorders in other parts of the body. As symptoms in the elderly are sometimes more difficult to diagnose, it is important that any changes, no matter how minor or unimportant they

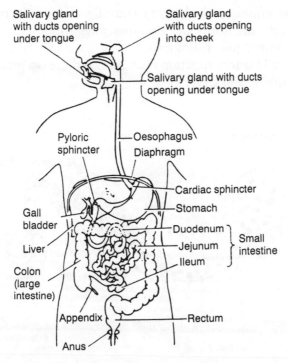

Fig 5.11 A healthy digestive system

may seem, are referred to a doctor or nurse. Symptoms which could indicate underlying disease include:

- loss of appetite
- weight loss
- diarrhoea
- nausea and vomiting
- pain and indigestion
- any other changes from the individual's normal bodily routine.

This section will examine signs, symptoms, causes, treatments and possible underlying causes of various digestive disorders that may affect the elderly. The term, digestive system, includes the mouth, the stomach, the intestines and also the digestive juices that are secreted during the process of digestion.

Though digestive disorders are common at any age, their incidence increases as the ageing process progresses. The process of ageing is discussed more fully in Chapter 3, but it would be helpful here to summarise exactly how these changes affect the digestive system.

- Muscles lose their elasticity and become less efficient at their work. This directly affects the muscular walls lining the alimentary canal which take longer to push the food along.

- Nerve impulses take longer to travel, so the production of gastric juices and relevant hormones becomes sluggish.
- The gastric juices diminish.
- The gall bladder function changes and there is a greater likelihood that gall-stones will develop.

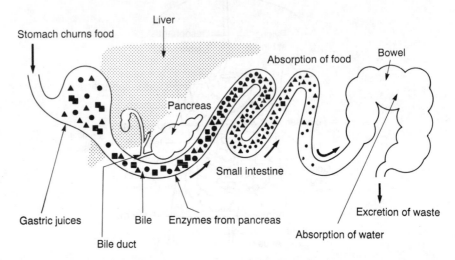

Fig 5.12 Plan of the passage of food along the alimentary canal, showing where the main digestive events occur during passage

An awareness of these changes is important as making changes earlier in life can help to avoid health problems developing in old age. For example:

- A high-fibre diet will help to reduce the constipation which frequently results from the loss of elasticity in the intestinal muscles.
- Eating smaller, more digestible meals will help reduce the burden on a system which is likely to be less able to cope with rich foods.
- Refer any problems to a doctor and avoid dosing up on over-the-counter medicines for digestive ailments without checking with the pharmacist first.

General symptoms

Abdominal pain

This can be:

- general or localised
- caused by a particular action such as eating, drinking, stress and so on
- either permanent or may come and go
- sharp or dull and cramp-like.

Dysphagia

This is difficulty in swallowing and can have a number of causes.

Indigestion

This is the umbrella term used to describe a number of different symptoms resulting from eating. These symptoms range from pain anywhere along the digestive tract to flatulence. Some of the causes of these symptoms include ulcers, hiatus hernias and gastritis. Indigestion is common in all age groups, affecting around three in ten of the general population, but this figure rises to about five in ten among the elderly.

The following are the most common causes of indigestion.

- **Hiatus hernia**. This occurs when the reduced elasticity of the opening in the diaphragm which allows the oesophagus becomes enlarged and lets part of the stomach come up into the chest. This means that the stomach acids cause soreness and inflammation in that area.

  The treatment is to raise the bedhead, reduce the size of meals, and to take prescribed antacids. If these fail, surgery may be necessary.

- **Ulcers** of the stomach or duodenum result from the erosion of the walls in these areas. Severe ulcers can eat through the walls and cause peritonitis. Most ulcers are easily cured by various drugs and by avoiding things such as smoking, drinking alcohol or taking aspirin-based drugs.

- The likelihood of **gall-stones** forming increases with age. The symptoms are pain and nausea, especially after eating greasy food, and vomiting. Doctors prefer to avoid surgery in the elderly unless the case is too severe to respond to first stage treatment which is to lose weight and avoid fatty foods.

Diarrhoea

As this is the most common disorder it is also the most difficult to diagnose. The signs are pain and loose motions. Usually the condition cures itself and the sufferer need only maintain liquid intake and cut down on food.

Prolonged diarrhoea causes more concern. The most likely causes of this condition in the elderly are listed below.

- **Diverticular disease** results when small bubbles of the intestinal lining pop through the muscular intestinal wall. These bubbles are called diverticula and are likely to become inflamed when faecal material collects in them.

  The main symptoms are diarrhoea, constipation, bleeding and abdominal pain on the lower left side. The treatment is a high fibre diet and antibiotics.

- **Over-indulgence** in food or drink, taking either prescribed or self-prescribed drugs, and anxiety can also cause diarrhoea.

- **Ulcerative colitis**, a chronic inflammation of the large bowel, has symptoms of pain and bloody diarrhoea. Treatment involving steroids to reduce the inflammation and a diet free of fruit may be sufficient to cure the condition. In severe cases, however, an ileostomy may be necessary. This involves surgically removing the large bowel and brining the small bowel, the ileum, out at an opening in the abdomen where the faecal material is collected in a bag.

- **Crohn's disease**, which is an inflammatory condition of the ileum, has symptoms of diarrhoea, loss of appetite, fever, weight loss and pain. The condition can lead to ulceration, causing further complications. Treatment is by antidiarrhoeal drugs, water-absorbing bulking agents or steroids.
- **Gastritis**, which is the inflammation of the stomach lining, can be either acute or chronic. Acute gastritis is generally a reaction to something either eaten or drunk and its symptoms are nausea, diarrhoea, vomiting and blood in the vomit. Chronic gastritis, which is more likely in the elderly, has less obvious symptoms. The condition is caused by the breakdown of the stomach lining as a result of ageing.

Constipation

Constipation is a change in the normal bowel patterns of an individual. It is quite normal for some people to pass a motion every other day while others may normally pass a motion daily. There are no set rules about frequency of bowel movement – constipation means a change from the individual's own norm. The sufferer experiences discomfort or pain when trying to empty the bowel of hard stools and there are usually fewer stools than normal.

The most common causes of constipation in the elderly are:

- too little fibre in the diet
- lack of exercise, often as a result of being bedridden
- the side effects of certain drugs such as antidepressants and painkillers, especially those derived from codeine, and the overuse of laxatives
- underactive thyroid (myxodema)
- obstruction of the bowel.

It is possible that constipation could eventually lead to faecal impaction, which is when the hardening stools block the bowel, usually the rectum. As a result of this, only fluid and loose stools can pass by the blockage and they will leak out. This condition may be mistaken for diarrhoea.

The best treatment for constipation is to:

- eat high fibre foods
- exercise as much as possible
- open the bowels promptly, as soon as the message is received
- avoid over-the-counter laxatives.

Faecal incontinence

One of the causes of this condition is faecal impaction which has already been discussed. The other is when the message from the brain warning of the need to open the bowels passes unrecognised, for example as a result of a stroke or confusional condition.

Treatment takes the form of either diagnosing and treating any underlying cause or, if the condition is likely to be permanent, managing it. As a last resort, it may be necessary to give enemas or use incontinence pads.

Other disorders of the digestive system

Cancer of the stomach, oesophagus, or bowel

These cancers make up quite a high proportion of cancer cases. Cancer is not one disease, it is a disorder of cell-growth in a particular part of the body. Cancer cells invade other, healthy cells and destroy them.

There are various factors that increase the likelihood of developing cancer which are discussed in more detail later, but the elderly are more at risk simply because their body tissues are ageing.

The symptoms of **stomach cancer** are:

- pain in the abdomen
- loss of weight and appetite
- vomiting, possibly with blood
- anaemia.

The causes are not completely understood, but the likelihood of contracting stomach cancer is increased if the sufferer has:

- pernicious anaemia
- gastric ulcers
- smoked
- atrophic gastritis.

Because the early symptoms often pass unnoticed, the disease is likely to cause death within four years.

The symptoms of **bowel cancer** are:

- blood or mucus in the stools
- a change in bowel habits, i.e. constipation, diarrhoea, faecal incontinence
- abdominal pain
- loss of weight and appetite
- anaemia.

One of the major contributory factors in bowel cancer is thought to be the high level of fat, sugar, salt and processed food in the western diet. If the condition is caught early and treated, then the sufferer has a good outlook.

The symptoms of **oesophagal cancer** are:

- an increased difficulty in swallowing
- sudden weight loss.

Contributory factors are thought to be smoking and drinking.

Mouth disorders

There are many reasons why the elderly are likely to suffer from sore mouths, these are:

- dehydration leading to a dry mouth
- poor teeth or ill-fitting dentures
- ulcers
- reaction to some drug treatments
- vitamin deficiencies
- anaemia
- thrush.

It is important that the cause is diagnosed to prevent the sufferer from developing further symptoms.

Cirrhosis of the liver

This is caused by decay or injury to the liver. The liver cells become irreversibly damaged and are replaced by hard and nodular tissue. If caught in time, the tissues can regenerate themselves.

Cirrhosis may result from:

- severe alcoholism
- blockage of the bile duct
- viral hepatitis, type B
- chemical damage.

The symptoms of cirrhosis are:

- pale, lifeless complexion
- loss of weight and appetite
- anaemia
- tingling hands and feet
- feeling of ill-health.

Haemorrhoids

Haemorrhoids are varicose veins of the rectum and can be either internal or external. They are caused by pelvic pressure, which can be a result of:

- constipation
- in women the condition often starts during pregnancy
- coughing
- overuse of laxatives or enemas.

If the condition deteriorates, other symptoms can develop:

- bleeding, which can cause anaemia
- localised thrombosis, which is painful
- pruritis
- fungal infection.

Treatments include:

- suppositories or ointments applied to the haemorrhoids
- injections to shrink them
- surgery to remove them
- to treat the underlying cause, i.e. if it is constipation, then change to a high fibre diet; if it is a cough, then seek the cause of the cough, and so on.

Disorders of the urino-genital system

In old age the tissues lose their elasticity, and this affects the bladder by reducing its capacity to roughly half that of a younger person. Messages from the brain take longer to be relayed in the elderly which may result in the message of needing to empty the bladder not being recognised until the bladder is virtually full.

Stress incontinence, when urine escapes during laughing, coughing, sneezing, exercising and so on, is relatively common in older women, often occurring as a result of childbirth.

Other causes of incontinence in the elderly are listed below.

Urinary tract infections

These are so-called when the bacterial content of the urine reaches a certain level.

The symptoms of this condition are:

- frequency of micturation (passing water)
- burning pain when passing water
- sometimes a feeling of being unwell
- urine may be cloudy and fishy smelling.

Bacteria in the urine of the elderly is not in itself a problem unless it is the symptom of an underlying disease.

One of the most common urinary tract infections is **cystitis**, which affects women more than men for the following reasons:

- the urethra is short and, therefore, more likely to be affected by intercourse, injury or infection
- the area may have been previously damaged by pregnancy and childbirth
- the urethra is closer to the anus so is more likely to become infected.

Urinary tract infections are more likely in the following circumstances:

- lack of personal hygiene
- an unclean environment caused by, for instance, poverty
- diabetes
- the presence of kidney stones
- prostate problems in men.

Enlarged prostate gland

The prostate gland is situated below the bladder and has the urethra passing through it. Its function is to produce the lubricating fluid used to transport the sperm during intercourse. Sometimes the gland becomes enlarged which obstructs, or may completely block, the flow of urine.

The symptoms of an enlarged prostate gland are:

- hesitant urination
- small amounts of urine passed
- frequency of micturation, especially in the night
- the feeling that the bladder hasn't emptied
- prolonged and painful erections.

The cause of this condition is not known, but is thought by some to be caused by too little sexual activity. Other contributory factors are the growth of small cysts on the gland, alcohol and bladder infections.

In more serious cases, the cure is to remove the prostate gland, which does not affect the man's libido or sexual performance. Often the condition may have been the result of unusual factors such as over-indulgence in alcohol, or taking certain drugs, so will pass. Surgery is always riskier in older people, so a permanent catheter may be used instead.

Loss of bladder control

A lack of response to messages from a full bladder may be the result of confusional states. In a mentally healthy person, however, it can signify a neurological disorder such as multiple sclerosis or spinal damage. In some women the condition can be caused by hormonal imbalance and can be cured by hormone replacement therapy (HRT).

Many cases of loss of bladder control can be treated, but if the cause is untreatable, then continence management, using either a catheter or incontinence aids will need to be implemented (see Chapter 11).

Disorders of the eyes

Any disorder that reduces the efficiency of the eye increases the likelihood of accident and injury. More importantly, and this fact is often overlooked, loss of sight affects our ability to communicate effectively with other people. It is therefore very important to have regular eye check-ups so that any problems can be dealt with as soon as possible.

The cells in the retina collect the images and transmit them to the brain where they are then interpreted. Partial or complete loss of sight affects our ability to make sense of our surroundings.

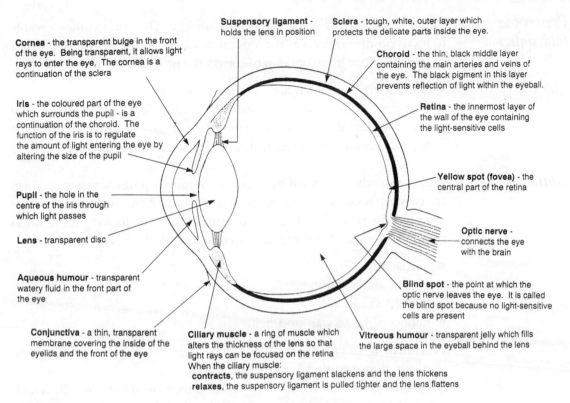

Cornea - the transparent bulge in the front of the eye. Being transparent, it allows light rays to enter the eye. The cornea is a continuation of the sclera

Iris - the coloured part of the eye which surrounds the pupil - is a continuation of the choroid. The function of the iris is to regulate the amount of light entering the eye by altering the size of the pupil

Pupil - the hole in the centre of the iris through which light passes

Lens - transparent disc

Aqueous humour - transparent watery fluid in the front part of the eye

Suspensory ligament - holds the lens in position

Sclera - tough, white, outer layer which protects the delicate parts inside the eye.

Choroid - the thin, black middle layer containing the main arteries and veins of the eye. The black pigment in this layer prevents reflection of light within the eyeball.

Retina - the innermost layer of the wall of the eye containing the light-sensitive cells

Yellow spot (fovea) - the central part of the retina

Optic nerve - connects the eye with the brain

Blind spot - the point at which the optic nerve leaves the eye. It is called the blind spot because no light-sensitive cells are present

Conjunctiva - a thin, transparent membrane covering the inside of the eyelids and the front of the eye

Ciliary muscle - a ring of muscle which alters the thickness of the lens so that light rays can be focused on the retina
When the ciliary muscle:
　contracts, the suspensory ligament slackens and the lens thickens
　relaxes, the suspensory ligament is pulled tighter and the lens flattens

Vitreous humour - transparent jelly which fills the large space in the eyeball behind the lens

Fig 5.13 Diagram of a horizontal section through a right eye as seen from above a right eye because of the direction for the optic nerve

General changes in the ageing eyes are:

- eyesight becomes less acute
- colour discrimination is less accurate
- the eyes take longer to adjust to changes in light intensity.

There are, however, some eye disorders that are more likely to develop in old age.

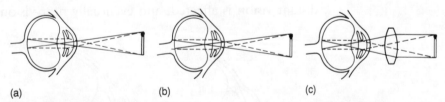

(a) (b) (c)

Fig 5.14 (a) Normal eyesight. The eye focuses on the matchstick and the image is projected upside down and back to front on the retina. The brain puts the image the right way up.
(b) Longsight (presbyopia). The lens is less able to change shape so the image falls behind the retina.
(c) Corrective glasses. Opticians prescribe glasses with lenses that curve outwards making the image fall on to the retina.

Presbyopia (old sight)

This condition tends to develop in middle-age. The eye becomes less able to focus on near objects as the lens takes longer to alter its shape. Glasses can be prescribed by an optician to correct the problem. These can either be:

- reading glasses, which are only used for close work
- bi-focals, which have two lenses; the reading lens at the bottom and the long-distance lens on top. These type of glasses take longer to adjust to, but remove the need to keep taking glasses on and off.

Glaucoma

This is a condition caused by pressure building up inside the eye. There are two types of glaucoma: acute and chronic. **Acute glaucoma** results in a very narrow angle of vision so the sufferer ends up looking at the world through a tunnel. The symptoms come on suddenly and are:

- headache
- nausea and vomiting
- blurred vision
- rainbow-like arcs around lights.

Treatment is an emergency operation to relieve the pressure. Blindness results if the condition is left untreated.

Chronic glaucoma is caused by a gradual increase in pressure which leads to an often unnoticeable loss of peripheral vision. If left untreated the sufferer will eventually become completely blind.

Unlike the symptoms of acute glaucoma, the gradual loss of vision symptomatic of chronic glaucoma may pass unnoticed for many years which means irreversible damage will occur. The treatment after diagnosis is to either prescribe drops that relieve the pressure or recommend an operation.

There is no way of preventing glaucoma, so regular eye tests are vital. For chronic glaucoma, however, there is evidence that it runs in the family.

Cataracts

Cataracts form on the lens making it opaque and affecting vision. At first, distant vision is affected, and eventually near vision.

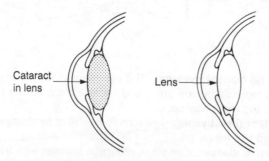

Cataract in lens

Lens

Fig 5.15 **Diagram showing a normal lens and one with a cataract**

Cataracts are usually caused by an inefficient blood supply to the lens, but they can be the result of diabetes, glaucoma or other eye disorders.

Cataracts cannot be cured, but have to be surgically removed. After the operation, which can be performed under local or general anaesthetic, the sufferer will need to have either glasses, lens implants or contact lenses to replace the removed lens.

Disorders of the ears

The ear is divided into three sections; the outer, middle and inner ear. The functions of the outer and middle ears are to collect and conduct sound to the inner ear where the auditory nerve will transmit the sound messages to the brain. The inner ear also contains the organs of balance.

Complete or partial hearing loss not only prevents the sufferer from communicating with others, it also means that the person is unlikely to hear signs of danger. Hearing loss in the elderly is quite common. Acute

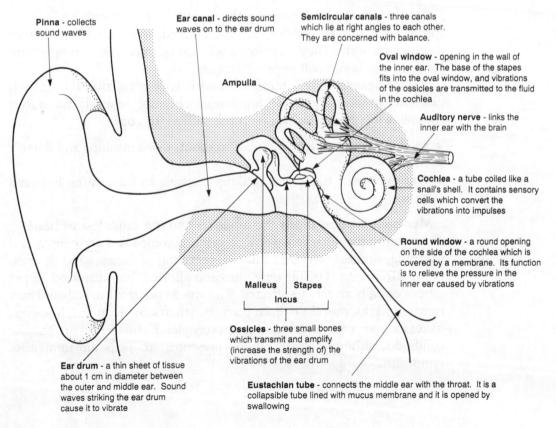

Pinna - collects sound waves

Ear canal - directs sound waves on to the ear drum

Semicircular canals - three canals which lie at right angles to each other. They are concerned with balance.

Oval window - opening in the wall of the inner ear. The base of the stapes fits into the oval window, and vibrations of the ossicles are transmitted to the fluid in the cochlea

Ampulla

Auditory nerve - links the inner ear with the brain

Cochlea - a tube coiled like a snail's shell. It contains sensory cells which convert the vibrations into impulses

Round window - a round opening on the side of the cochlea which is covered by a membrane. Its function is to relieve the pressure in the inner ear caused by vibrations

Malleus   Stapes

Incus

Ossicles - three small bones which transmit and amplify (increase the strength of) the vibrations of the ear drum

Ear drum - a thin sheet of tissue about 1 cm in diameter between the outer and middle ear. Sound waves striking the ear drum cause it to vibrate

Eustachian tube - connects the middle ear with the throat. It is a collapsible tube lined with mucus membrane and it is opened by swallowing

Fig 5.16 Structure of the ear

hearing diminishes with age, and the ability to hear high-pitched sounds is lost first. It also becomes increasingly difficult to differentiate between sounds, especially when there is a lot of background noise.

The amount of wax in the ears increases and hardens, often as a result of upper respiratory tract infections, and tends to block the ears. Wax can easily be treated by applying ear drops for a few days to soften the build up of wax and then syringeing the ears clean.

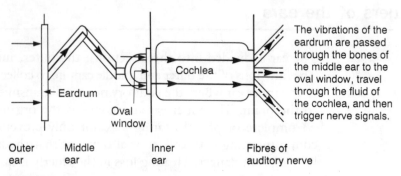

The vibrations of the eardrum are passed through the bones of the middle ear to the oval window, travel through the fluid of the cochlea, and then trigger nerve signals.

Cochlea

Eardrum

Oval window

Outer ear | Middle ear | Inner ear | Fibres of auditory nerve

Fig 5.17 How sound passes through the ear

Occasionally the small bones in the middle ear that transfer the sounds to the inner ear, the **ossicles**, become calcified, so are unable to convey sounds effectively. They may also be affected by infections. An operation to free these bones will improve hearing.

Loss of hearing is very traumatic and it is essential that the cause is diagnosed as soon as possible. Sometimes a hearing aid will be fitted, but the following guidelines will help the sufferer to cope:

- speak clearly but there is no need to shout; this is insulting and doesn't help
- find out about the special facilities available to the hearing impaired person.

Meniere's disease affects the inner ear and can cause loss of hearing. The symptoms are severe vertigo, often accompanied by nausea and vomiting, tinnitus (noises in the ear), flickering of the eyes and deafness in the affected ear. Usually only one ear is affected, but in around 15 per cent of cases, both ears are affected. The attacks occur at intervals and may recur for weeks, months or even years, and then stop. Deafness, however, increases with each attack and is irreversible. There is no cure for the condition, although drugs can be prescribed to help the immediate symptoms.

Disorders of the teeth

Teeth are not only used to chew food, they are also needed to help form speech sounds. In the western world around half of all 65 year-olds have lost many of their teeth. The causes are lack of care and a diet high in sugars.

The common stereotype of an old person shows them toothless, chewing on empty gums and lisping when they talk. This stereotype need not be a reality. There are many cosmetic treatments that can make teeth look good and work well. Even sets of complete dentures do not need to cause problems if they are well-fitted and cared for. As always, it is essential to have regular check-ups to catch any potential problems before they become chronic.

In the past dentists tended to remove all the teeth for what now seem very minor reasons. Modern dentistry acknowledges the value of retaining teeth for as long as possible, sometimes going to extraordinary lengths to save a tooth. Should it become necessary to remove some teeth, it is felt that any remaining teeth will be useful to attach dentures to, thus aiding secure fitting.

Disorders of the skin

As was discussed in Chapter 3, the skin is the most obvious sign of an ageing body. It loses its elasticity and becomes drier, causing the characteristic lines and wrinkles of old age. The skin cells do not replace themselves as often as in youth and there is less underlying tissue, so the skin is thinner and becomes more likely to show broken blood vessels under its surface.

The skin develops more blemishes as it ages, the following being particularly associated with old age:

- **Moles**. These are areas of pigmentation and are usually harmless. However, any changes in their number or size and shape etc. should be reported to a doctor.
- **Brown spots** (commonly known as age spots) increase with age and are harmless. They are more often to be found on areas that are exposed to the sun.
- Little red spots – **macules** – are found on the trunk and are also harmless.
- **Seborrhoeic warts** are raised brown or black areas measuring up to one inch across. Again, they are not dangerous.
- **Skin tags**, small painless tags of skin, are another harmless skin blemish common in old age. They are often found on the neck and affect women more than men. Though not dangerous, they may be easily removed by a doctor for cosmetic reasons.

Although there are other skin disorders that may affect the elderly, their incidence in old age is no higher than in any other age group.

Intertrigo

This condition develops in areas of skin which are in contact, such as the groin area. The symptoms are inflammation and an unpleasant smell. It develops as a result of moisture, either sweat or urine, creating friction between the areas of skin which leads to infection.

Treatment is to bath regularly, dry the skin well and use talcum powder. If this is not a success, an ointment may be prescribed to apply to the infected area.

Psoriasis

This is a skin disease which the elderly person may well have had all their lives. It is recognised by a series of red scaly areas which may be itchy and, depending on the severity of the condition, prone to bleeding if knocked. In some cases the disease may be accompanied by arthritis.

There is no cure but the symptoms may be controlled by a range of different treatments, depending on the degree of the problem. These treatments include coal tar or dithranol ointments, steroids, or even admission to hospital in extreme cases where large areas of skin are involved.

Shingles

Shingles, or herpes zoster, is linked to the chicken pox virus. The condition is caused by a dormant chicken pox virus which becomes activated if the person's general health is low. The symptoms are pain in an area of the body – often the chest – followed by the appearance of blisters a few days later, fever and a feeling of illness.

Anti-viral treatments are available to help reduce the severity of the attack.

Pemphigus

This is a potentially life-threatening condition if left untreated. Its symptoms are large blisters in areas of the body where there is friction, e.g. the groin, between the buttocks, the armpits and, occasionally, in the mouth, and the sufferer feels ill. The cause is unknown and the condition, fortunately rare, can be treated with steroids.

Ulceration of the legs

This is a common condition in the elderly and is caused by bad circulation. The symptoms are weeping, open ulcers measuring up to inches across. They are painless unless they become infected, but left untreated they may last indefinitely.

Treatment involves regular cleaning of the ulcer and a reduction of the swelling. The leg should not be over-used, and raised when resting. In severe cases it may be necessary to resort to surgery and perform a skin graft.

Skin cancer

Skin cancer usually develops on areas of skin which have been most exposed to sunlight, particularly the face. There are different types of skin cancer.

Basal-cell carcinoma, or rodent ulcer, is found on the neck, nose, ears and eyelids. It does not spread to other parts of the body and is easily treated by surgical removal or radiotherapy.

Squamous cell carcinoma is a series of hard growths usually found on the face and neck. If the area is treated, this condition is also unlikely to spread.

Malignant melanoma is a rarer form of skin cancer and usually develops on the site of an existing mole. If left untreated it will spread to other parts of the body, which is why it is important to report any changes in moles and so on to a doctor.

Scalp and hair conditions
The scalp and hair change with ageing, with the hair growing more slowly and being thinner, as well as losing its pigmentation. Body hair is also lost from the armpits and pubic areas. Women will develop facial hair. The scalp may be affected by any or all of the following conditions.

- Baldness, usually in men, but elderly women will also suffer. The cause may be the ageing process, a reaction to certain drugs or treatments, or alopecia areata.
- Dandruff.
- Parasites.
- Psoriasis.
- Shingles.

It is very important to take good care of the hair and scalp. There are many old wives' tales about the dangers of over-washing the hair and so on, but regular washing can help both to prevent certain conditions from developing and to spot potential problems.

Hormonal disorders

Most hormonal problems begin in middle-age rather than old age, the most common hormonal disorders are diabetes and thyroid gland dysfunctions.

Diabetes
There are two types of diabetes. The first is caused by the inability of the pancreas to produce insulin and can affect an individual at any age. The second type is more likely to develop in old age and is caused by less insulin being produced, leading to an excess of sugar in the blood stream.

There is evidence that the following factors may increase a person's chances of developing this second type of diabetes:

- ageing
- a family history of the condition
- obesity.

There is also a risk of conditions such as chronic kidney disease or atherosclerosis being exacerbated by diabetes. Damaged blood vessels may increase the likelihood of disorders arising from poor circulation. The eyes, too, are likely to be affected.

Often, the type of diabetes associated with ageing can be controlled by:

- diet, i.e. by limiting daily carbohydrate intake
- by taking tablets.

In addition to this treatment, a diabetic should keep a regular check on the following:

- eyesight
- feet, by visiting a chiropodist regularly
- any injuries, however slight they may seem.

Thyroid gland dysfunctions

The most common thyroid gland problems are an under-active thyroid, **hypothyroidism,** or an over-active thyroid, **thyrotoxicosis.**

Thyrotoxicosis is less common in the elderly and is not easily diagnosed as the symptoms are different. The symptoms are weight loss, heart

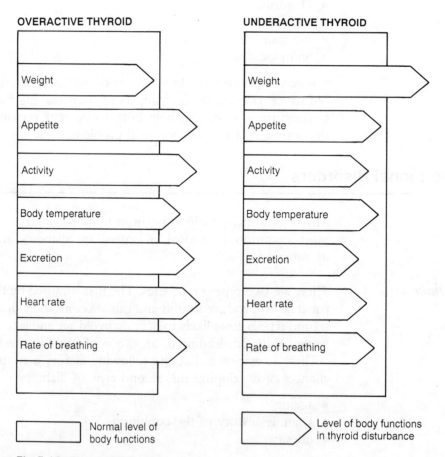

Fig 5.18 **The thyroid gland**

palpitations and sometimes depression. Once diagnosed, the treatment is quite simple, but the condition needs to be checked regularly throughout life.

Hypothyroidism often goes unrecognised and the symptoms – loss of memory, sluggishness, feeling cold, deepening voice, deafness and puffy face – are often put down to ageing, especially as the onset is gradual.

Disorders affecting the nervous system

The nervous system is also affected by ageing (*see* Chapter 3). The brain governs the nervous system so, when it is damaged in any way, the mind or body functions will suffer.

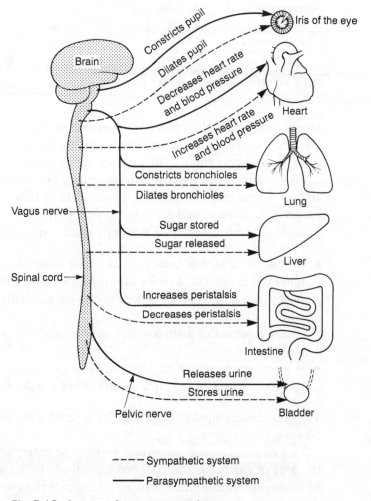

Fig 5.19 Autonomic nervous system

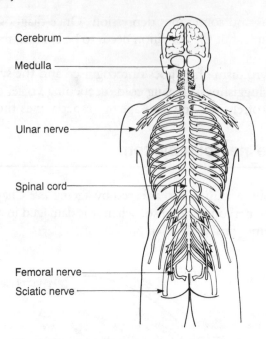

Cerebrum

Medulla

Ulnar nerve

Spinal cord

Femoral nerve
Sciatic nerve

Fig 5.20 The human nervous system

Strokes

Strokes are one of the most common causes of cerebrovascular disease in the western world. The older the person, the more likely they are to suffer from strokes and the less likely they are to make a full recovery.

Strokes are caused by either haemorrhages or blood clots which starve an area of the brain of oxygen. This area then dies and is, therefore, no longer able to carry out its original function.

Strokes take a number of different forms and vary in severity.

- Transient ischaemic attacks may cause temporary disability, such as blindness in one eye, a drooping eyelid, difficulty with speech or paralysis of the side of the mouth which comes on suddenly and may disappear within a day.
- The symptoms of a stroke may appear gradually and continue to get worse.
- A severe stroke where the victim may lose consciousness and suffer from paralysis. There is a greater likelihood of death in this type of stroke.

The less serious strokes can often be treated if an underlying cause can be found.

Strokes are classified according to their severity, and this depends on the area of the brain affected. Strokes caused by a haemorrhage tend to be more serious than those caused by a clot as the blood can cause a great deal of brain damage. The onset of these strokes is often sudden. The type of stroke caused by a blood clot offers a greater hope of recovery.

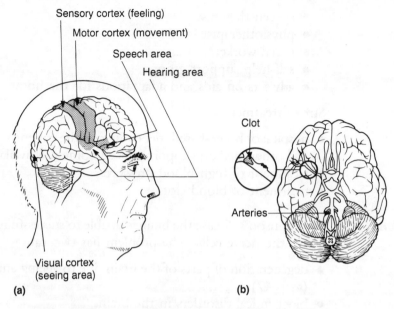

Fig 5.21 (a) Functions governed by different areas of the brain (b) A brain clot or haemorrhage may cause a stroke

Stroke damage may include:

- complete paralysis
- paralysis of one side of the body – hemiplegia
- paralysis of one arm or one leg – monoplegia
- loss of sensation down one side of the body – hemianaesthesia
- loss of half the field of vision – hemianopia
- speech slurring – dysarthria
- complex changes in speech patterns that are apparent to the listener but not to the stroke victim, known as aphasia
- difficulty in swallowing – dysphagia.

The management of stroke-induced disability has improved in recent years, and tends to follow a general pattern:

1 Assessment to both diagnose and look at the possible causes in order to work out a programme of rehabilitation based on the severity of the stroke.
2 Putting the rehabilitation programme into practice.
3 Counselling to help with the sufferer's mental reaction to the stroke.
4 Help and support for the family, including involving them in the rehabilitation programme.
5 Long-term support from any of the following:
   - doctor
   - nurse
   - occupational therapist

- speech therapist
- physiotherapist
- social worker
- self-help support groups
- advisers on aids and adaptations for the home.

Stroke treatment can be:

- hospital or home-based, depending on the patient's condition. Nursing and other medical support plus equipment is available for home care.
- treatment of high blood pressure.
- treatment of blood clots.

Parkinson's disease

In Parkinson's disease the brain is unable to successfully transmit messages across the nerve cells. The problem has two causes:

- degeneration of parts of the brain due to ageing and, often, atheroma (*see* p 47)
- biochemical disorders in the brain.

The symptoms of the disease are:

- tremor which makes certain actions difficult
- slowness of movement
- muscular stiffness
- lack of armswing when walking
- expressionless face
- body leaning forward
- small, shuffling steps.

Later symptoms may include:

- excess of saliva
- greasy and sweaty skin
- difficulty with talking
- difficulty in swallowing
- increased inability to perform everyday tasks.

More recently there has been an improvement in the treatment of Parkinson's disease sufferers, although there is still no cure. The drug, L-dopa, has improved the condition of sufferers by relieving the brain's chemical imbalance. The sufferer will also need help from physiotherapy and occupational therapy to re-learn skills such as walking.

Motor neurone disease

This disorder is a progressive wasting of the muscles, usually those of the hands, legs, tongue or throat. The muscles can either become stiff or will twitch under the skin's surface. Mental faculties are not affected.

The disease is potentially fatal if the throat and/or tongue is affected as the sufferer will either choke, or develop pneumonia as a result of food going into the lungs. If the legs are affected there is a better outlook for the sufferer.

There is no cure for the disease, but there are ways of managing the symptoms:

- physiotherapy
- occupational therapy
- help with mobility
- home aids and adaptations
- liquidising food to reduce the likelihood of choking.

Potential health disorders

There are other potential disorders that are more likely to affect the elderly.

Anaemia

There can be various causes of anaemia:

- iron-deficiency in the blood often caused by internal bleeding
- pernicious anaemia caused by vitamin B12 deficiency
- folic acid deficiency, often caused by a poor diet
- bone marrow and other diseases which affect the haemoglobin levels in the blood
- sickle-cell anaemia, which is an inherited condition found mainly in black people. The symptoms start in childhood and continue throughout life.

The symptoms of anaemia are:

- tiredness
- shortness of breath
- dizziness
- paleness
- loss of appetite
- headaches
- sleeplessness
- palpitations
- swelling of the ankles
- chest pains.

The treatment depends on the type of anaemia the person is suffering from:

- iron-deficiency anaemia can be treated with iron capsules or injections
- pernicious anaemia can be treated by a course of vitamin B12 injections. More serious cases may need a blood transfusion
- folic acid deficiency anaemia can be treated with folic acid tablets
- for anaemia caused by underlying disease the treatment depends on diagnosing the disease, and its successful treatment. The condition can be helped, however, by iron and folic acid tablets
- sickle-cell anaemia is usually treated by regular blood transfusions.

Dehydration

Dehydration is more likely in the elderly for any of the following reasons:

- not taking in enough fluids
- diarrhoea or sickness
- as a result of taking diuretic drugs
- reduced efficiency of the kidneys which become less able to conserve salt and water.

The symptoms of dehydration are:

- weakness
- tiredness
- low blood pressure.

It is important to make sure that fluid intake is kept up, even if the person is worried about needing to visit the toilet frequently.

Acute kidney failure

Acute kidney failure can be caused by chronic kidney failure, dehydration, an obstruction to the flow of urine and other causes.

The symptoms are general feelings of illness, anaemia, a chemical imbalance of the urine and a fall in blood pressure.

Hypothermia

Hypothermia is when the body's core temperature falls to 35°C or below. It seems that the body becomes unable to maintain its temperature for the following reasons:

- Illness, such as pneumonia or a stroke, or a fall when the person is unable to get up because of injury.
- The cold. Often the elderly will not put the heating on either because of poverty, poor housing, or habit.
- A defect in homeostasis when the person may not be aware of the cold.

The treatment of hypothermia is to gradually bring the body's core temperature back to normal, and this needs hospitalisation. The interim treatment is to wrap the person in a blanket and warm the room; hot drinks should never be given.

A final note

Generally, all physical disorders can be helped in some way, even if they are not curable. Quality of life is vital, and no symptoms should be regarded as just a part of the ageing process.

Treatment of symptoms, however, is not always enough; many physical disorders require follow-up care and counselling, especially if the condition is likely to deteriorate. Tact and sympathy are the fundamental requirements of good treatment.

Key issues – a summary

- As the body ages it is more likely to develop health disorders.

- The likelihood of developing certain diseases may be set in younger life.

- Health disorders may be more difficult to diagnose in the elderly for various reasons.

- It is important to seek medical advice as soon as possible because the sooner a disease is diagnosed the earlier treatment can be started.

- Osteoarthritis is a common form of arthritis in old age. There is no known cure although symptoms can be treated.

- Rheumatoid arthritis can be more debilitating, although the severity of the disease varies. There is no cure.

- Loss of mobility can be caused by:
  - Diseases affecting the bones
  - Neurological diseases
  - Strokes
  - Circulatory problems
  - Foot disorders
  - Impairment of the sense of balance.

- Atherosclerosis accounts for almost half of all deaths in the western world, but the number of deaths could be reduced if people changed their lifestyles.

- The number of people dying from heart disease could be reduced by a change in lifestyle, although there are a number of contributory factors.

- Smoking, eating a diet high in salt, sugar and fats and low in fibre and drinking alcohol all increase the likelihood of developing heart disease.

- The efficiency of the lungs is reduced in old age.

- Living and working in a polluted atmosphere can increase the likelihood of developing lung disease.

- Pneumonia is quite common in the sick elderly population and is often the cause of death following a serious illness.

- Lung cancer is a common cause of death in the United Kingdom and is strongly linked to smoking.

- Although the elderly are more likely to suffer from digestive disorders, a healthy diet can help to minimise the problems.

- All digestive disorders should be referred to the GP if they don't improve quickly.

- Incontinence is a common problem in old age and it is important to diagnose the underlying cause.

- Loss of eyesight can cause injury and accidents, so it is important to have any disorder checked immediately.

- Loss of hearing increases the risk of accidental injury and makes communication difficult. Many of the causes of hearing loss can be treated.

- Skin disorders can be irritating, and some can be dangerous. It is important to refer any problems to the GP.

- Strokes are one of the most common causes of death in the western world. They are classified according to their severity. Lifestyle can affect the likelihood of suffering from a stroke.

- An elderly person who becomes too cold, is injured or ill, or who has a defect in their homeostasis, is likely to develop hypothermia.

- The elderly should never be satisfied with the belief that any health disorder is acceptable as it is part of ageing. Most disorders can be helped even if they cannot be cured.

- Treating illness in the elderly should not simply be a case of treating symptoms; there is a place for follow-up care and counselling.

Assignment 5 Ageing and physical health disorders

This chapter has looked at the symptoms, causes and treatment of many of the health disorders found in the elderly. In a general book on ageing, it is impractical to look at the disorders in any detail because of space limitations. It would, however, be useful to carry out your own, more detailed, research on each of the disorders outlined here as it would help your understanding.

TASK 1:
FINDING A CURE
FOR ARTHRITIS

As yet there is no known cure for arthritis. In the 1980s a drug called Opren, which had been hailed as a wonder drug for arthritis sufferers, was found to have had side-effects.

Look up the details about the Opren case and write a brief summary.

TASK 2:
AIDS FOR ARTHRITIS
SUFFERERS

Find out about the various aids and adaptations available for arthritis sufferers in the home, in the garden, at work and for leisure.

Here are some ideas of where to look for your information:

- Disabled Living Foundation
- Occupational Therapy Unit
- Arthritis group.

**TASK 3:
HRT AND
OSTEOPOROSIS**

Osteoporosis is more prevalent in women and many doctors believe that Hormone Replacement Therapy (HRT) is an effective treatment.

Find out about HRT. You will need to find out:
- what it is
- how it works
- the advantages and disadvantages
- how it can help osteoporosis sufferers.

**TASK 4:
ATHEROSCLEROSIS**

Look into the problem of atherosclerosis in more detail as it is a major cause of death in the western world.

You may wish to cover these points:

- a definition of the term
- possible causes
- treatment
- guidelines on lifestyle that will help avoid the likelihood of developing the disease.

**TASK 5:
MAIN FUNCTIONS
OF THE HEART**

Check that you understand the workings of the heart. If you are not sure, ask a medical professional or biology tutor to outline the main functions. Try also to get hold of either a model heart or a video to help make the explanation clearer.

**TASK 6:
HEART DISEASE**

Heart disease is considered to be one of the more avoidable diseases of the western world.

Look at the factors which are known to increase the risk of developing heart disease (p 50). For each factor, explain the risk.

**TASK 7:
AVOIDING HEART
DISEASE**

Many professionals who know about the causes of heart disease believe that young children should be educated about the dangers of an unhealthy lifestyle.

As a group, suggest ideas to educate school children about the dangers of heart disease in a way that makes it interesting. Write your ideas as a set of suggestions that could be used in a primary school.

**TASK 8:
HOW THE LUNGS
WORK**

Check that you understand the workings of the lungs. If you don't, then follow the procedure of Task 5.

**TASK 9:
CLEAN AIR**

Until the late 1950s, bronchitis and other lung diseases were very common because of the polluted air. It became illegal to burn anything other than smokeless fuel in London, and there were many other initiatives to clean up the air. The result was that lung diseases did diminish.

Research into the ways the air has been cleaned up since the 1950s.

TASK 10:
THE DIGESTIVE
SYSTEM

Check that you understand the workings of the digestive system. If you are not sure, follow the procedure for question 5.

TASK 11:
DIET FOR THE
ELDERLY

In the past the elderly were encouraged to eat a bland diet of steamed fish and lightly boiled eggs. Although things have changed for the better these days, there is still the idea that the elderly are like invalids.

Assuming that the person does not have a medical problem that requires a special diet, suggest a day's meals for an elderly couple.

TASK 12:
DEHYDRATION

Prolonged sickness and diarrhoea are potentially dangerous as they can cause dehydration.

Look into the signs, causes, treatment and dangers of dehydration and suggest ways it can be avoided during illness.

TASK 13:
CANCER

Cancer is a disease that can affect anybody at any age. It is a disease that strikes fear into people as it is associated with death. There are, however, many different types of cancer and treatment is becoming more successful.

Look into cancer. It may help you to use these headings:

- definition
- types
- causes
- treatment and its advantages and disadvantages
- research taking place
- preventive measures
- charities working on cancer research and support.

TASK 14:
EYE DISORDERS

Regular eye check ups are essential if eye diseases are to be treated early.

Write a set of facts about eyes which should cover these areas:

- brief outline of disorders affecting the eye
- long- and short-sightedness
- the problems of loss of sight
- how to get a check up, what happens and the cost
- help available for the blind or partially sighted in the community.

TASK 15:
LOSS OF HEARING

Hearing loss is not only dangerous as the sufferer may be unable to hear potential dangers, but it also affects the ability to communicate successfully.

Look at the help available both nationally and locally to help the elderly with hearing loss.

TASK 16:
SUFFERING A
STROKE

Strokes are at best debilitating and at worst fatal. Rehabilitation after a stroke takes time and patience.

Compile a set of guidelines that will help someone who has suffered a stroke, and their family, to cope with the situation. Your guidelines will need to cover:

- A definition of a stroke
- The effects it may have on the body and brain
- How the sufferer and the family will feel and possible avenues of help available both nationally and in the community
- Methods of rehabilitation and the personnel involved
- Aids and adaptations and financial help available
- Follow-up ideas.

TASK 17:
HYPOTHERMIA

Hypothermia is potentially fatal in the elderly. Look into the problems associated with hypothermia, which include:

- Lack of public awareness
- Lack of awareness in the elderly population
- Too little money to pay for heating.

As a group, discuss ways of overcoming these problem areas.

6 The caring services 1 – the social services

© John Birdsall Photography

The caring services are made up of a number of different statutory and voluntary agencies who liaise with each other in an attempt to provide for the needs of the elderly. These three chapters will look at the various agencies and the personnel involved in this provision.

There are three categories of care provision:

- **public sector** which is state funded
- **private sector** which has the overall aim of making a profit, so charges for its services
- **voluntary sector** which is run and funded by charities or non-profit-making organisations.

Care provision for the elderly may be provided by any one of the following statutory agencies:

- National Health Service, who provide health care
- Department of Health and Social Security, who provide financial services
- Social Services Department, who deal with people in need.

Statutory agencies are funded and operated by the state and exist by law. They also have statutory responsibilities for care. Additional care provision can be provided by the voluntary agencies. Nowadays, however, some would argue that voluntary care is becoming less an additional provision and more a necessary supplement to statutory sector provision, which is seen to be inadequate. Although some staff in these agencies may work on a voluntary basis, many of the employees are paid; the term voluntary refers more to the fact that the organisation is not set up as a result of a law, or statute.

Voluntary agencies may operate nationally, locally or in response to a particular problem or issue.

Some elderly people will pay to use private sector provision, either using their capital or the proceeds from insurance policies.

A brief history of the Welfare State

Before looking at statutory provision in detail, it will be helpful here to look at the meaning of the term, Welfare State.

The Welfare State was introduced to provide minimum standards of health, housing, education and income for the population from 'the cradle to the grave'. Before this provision, people in need had to rely on family, charity or the work house. The main laws which signalled the start of the Welfare State were:

1944 The Education Act, which said children had to attend full-time education up to the age of fifteen.

1946 National Health Service Act which created the National Health Service.

1946 National Assistance Act which gave financial help to the poor, sick, unemployed and disabled.

1948 Children's Act which aimed to bring all childcare under local authority control.

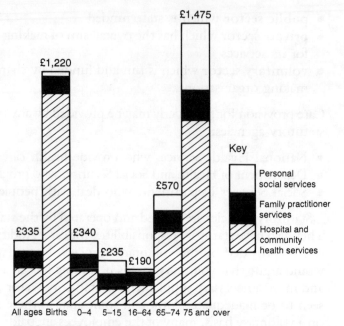

Fig 6.1 HPSS estimated gross current expenditure per head by age group (England), 1985–86

(*Source*: The Government Expenditure Plans 1988–9 HM Treasury 1988, HMSO. Reproduced by kind permission of HMSO. Crown Copyright)

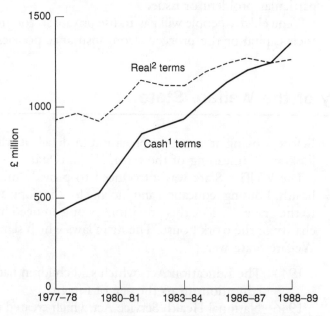

1   Cash figures are based on those published in Table 14.19 of the Public Expenditure White Paper (CM 614), January 1989.
2   Real terms figures are expressed in 1987–88 prices as adjusted by the GDP deflator published by HM Treasury in June 1989.

Fig 6.2 Capital expenditure on health (United Kingdom)

(Taken from *Social Trends 20*. Reproduced by kind permission of HMSO. Crown copyright 1990)

Since then there have been many changes in the Welfare State, but the basic aim to provide minimum standards of care still exists. The problem, however, seems to be reaching agreement on what constitutes 'minimum standards'.

The Social Services Department

The Social Services Department (SSD) comes under the auspices of the local authority. The Social Services Act of 1970 led to an integrated approach to provision for the elderly, children, the physically and mentally handicapped and the mentally ill.

The Barclay Report of 1982 made a number of recommendations about the way SSDs should be run with the following results:

- Long-term strategies became an integral part of social work planning. Many people felt this was a way of saving money while others described it as fairly distributing limited resources.
- The service was restructured and 'patch' teams of social workers were created with the aim of making the social worker more accessible to the client.
- The term 'community care' was introduced. The report felt that the SSD should make use of the family, friends, voluntary and private sector provision and local help by providing support for them. The implications of this for social workers were twofold:
  —to identify client needs, and
  —to make use of local resources to meet these needs.

Since this report there have been various new ideas and innovations and the service has gradually changed and adapted as each area decides what suits them best, or what they can afford. Following these changes, the SSDs could be described as having an 'enabling' role. This term was introduced in 1985 when the Government defined the SSD's role as being one of co-ordinating all the local provision and resources.

More recent changes aim to further implement the idea of community care and involve not only the family and friends, but also the private sector. There is an increasing emphasis on accountability and value-for-money. The implications of these changes are:

- SSDs will need to check on standards of private, public and voluntary sector provision, to check on 'value-for-money' in provision, and to deal with complaints arising from the introduction of increased accountability.
- Liaison will become both more vital and, as a result, more complex as so many different agencies could be involved in client care.

- Staff will need to keep abreast of a wealth of central government information relating to funding, social security payments, etc.
- Responsibility may become a more personal issue as people will be given specific roles and functions.

Why community care?

If you ask someone what they understand by the term 'community care' it is possible that you will receive two types of answer. The first may suggest that it is the type of care offered by the domiciliary support services, while the second may suggest that it is when the entire neighbourhood rallies around to help its needier members. The term is fraught with controversy because it involves issues of funding and care provision. It has, almost inevitably, become a political battleground, with both clients and carers feeling sometimes lost in the confusion. Against this background, the best approach is to examine the facts of the issue rather than the opinions.

The idea of community care, a term brought to the public's attention by the Barclay Report in 1982, began developing as long ago as the late 1950s when there was a reaction against long-term residential care. The arguments against long-term residential care were:

- The clients became institutionalised, which meant they lost much of their independence and initiative as a result of living in an institution.
- It was becoming increasingly difficult to find staff willing to work in residential homes.
- Improvements in drug treatment meant that there were fewer instances of behaviour that could be disturbing to society as a whole.
- The clients, although needing help, should not be ostracised by being shut away and had a right to be part of society.
- It was very expensive to keep people in residential care.

These arguments were gathering force throughout the 1960s and 1970s.

The Seebohm Report of 1968 emphasised that community care was not an unrealistic attempt to recreate a country village idyll of community but an attempt to involve the client group in making decisions about their care. The report went on to stress the need for using all provision within the community, which included family and friends as well as voluntary and statutory agencies.

The introduction of community care was further encouraged by the 1982 Barclay Report. In terms of policy-making decisions, the social services were seen as having a facilitating and co-ordinating role in initiatives that developed the idea of community care.

The effects of these changes on patterns of care for the elderly were:

- The number of residential homes was reduced.
- Sheltered accommodation was introduced as it offered care that was closer to normal housing.

- Only the elderly who were unable to care for themselves were taken into residential care.
- Help from family and friends was actively encouraged by social services provision.

The concept of community care changed the ethos of the care services: great changes were envisaged, but needed adequate funding and resources. As with all major changes, the issue is controversial. Critics would argue that:

- community care was introduced as a money-saving exercise, being described as 'cost-effective' by the DHSS 1981 Report of a study group on Community Care
- professionals in the care sector say that the service is under-funded
- families care for elderly relatives because they *have to* rather than *want to*, either because they would feel guilty asking for residential care or because existing facilities are often felt to be inadequate
- it is not possible to set or measure standards of care in a system that involves such a diversity of provision
- non-statutory provision, which had originally been intended to be complementary to statutory care provision, will increasingly become the main provider
- the burden of care usually falls on females
- evidence has shown that many elderly in the community are below the poverty line.

Proponents would argue that:

- community care is the responsibility of *all* the community and not just the government
- there is a great deal of untapped care potential in the community which should be used
- community care causes less disruption to the client's life and is less stressful
- it offers an opportunity to make use of all an area's resources
- community care enables the client to maintain a level of independence and a better quality of life.

The issue of community care is complex. There is no doubt that the idea is, in theory, a good one. In practice, however, its success relies on the provision of adequate resources, both human and financial.

The role and function of the Social Services Department

The director of social services, whose role is to run the Social Services Department, is appointed by the local authority social services committee.

It is the director's responsibility to provide adequate levels of statutory care within the budget restrictions imposed by the local authority. There will be variations in the level and standard of provision from area to area depending on the local authority's priorities and, to an extent, on the level of local taxation.

The main workload of the SSD is carried out by social workers. Social workers are usually generically trained, which means they are able to deal with all clients. However, as many social workers work in teams, some will specialise in a particular area of work which allows them to understand the area in more detail.

Social workers may work:

- 'in the field', when they may be attached to doctors' surgeries, hospitals, day centres and so on, or they could be based in the area offices
- in residential homes for children, the handicapped, the elderly, the mentally ill and so on.

Clients are put in touch with the social worker by a process called referral. Referrals of elderly clients may be made by:

- the client him/herself
- health services personnel
- family, friends or neighbours.

The client will then be visited so that an initial assessment can be made. The case will be referred on to the specialist social worker concerned with the relevant area of need.

The aims of SSD provision for the elderly

The overall aim of the social services, as we have seen, is to implement community care in order to help the elderly client to be independent for as long as possible.

The initial assessment will define the existing problems which could include any of the following:

- loneliness
- lack of money
- poor accommodation
- physical or mental ill-health
- neglect.

The social worker will recommend various ways of alleviating the problems. If the problems are too bad, they may recommend the client to residential care. In the rare cases when the client refuses to accept residential care, the social worker has the legal power to enforce admission.

The SSD has various types of support provision which can help the elderly client to maintain independence by living in their own home. To help alleviate loneliness there are:

- luncheon clubs
- day centres which may offer meals, socialisation and things to do
- mobile libraries provided through liaison with the library service
- holiday schemes.

To help with financial problems and deal with poor accommodation the SSD has welfare rights officers with specialist knowledge about allowances, who will tell their client the financial help available.

To help cope with ill-health, neglect, loss of mobility and frailty there are:

- meals-on-wheels, for which there is usually a small charge. These are delivered at lunchtimes, often by volunteers.
- home helps to help with housework and shopping. There may be a charge in some areas. Home helps are also a social contact.
- aids and adaptations which make it easier for the elderly with physical disabilities to go about their everyday lives. These may include bath rails, ramps, lifts and so on.
- night sitters are available in some areas. They may be used if there is a danger that the person's health will deteriorate or to give families a break from the responsibility of 24-hour care.
- day care, which is not the same as day centres. Day care is usually provided by a residential home for the elderly and offers transport to and from the centre and general care while there.

The SSD will continue to check on the client's progress by making regular visits. Should it become necessary to admit the elderly person to a residential home, the social worker has the responsibility of helping to make the move as easy as possible. This is done in consultation with the client and their family, Health Service personnel and staff of the residential home. If necessary, the client can be compulsorily admitted to residential care under Section 47 of the National Assistance Act 1948, but this is rare.

SSDs have a statutory responsibility to provide residential care for the elderly who are no longer able to cope in the community. Residential homes are called Part 111 accommodation as this requirement was set out under Part 111 of the National Assistance Act 1948.

Key issues – a summary

- The caring services are made up of a number of different agencies, both statutory and voluntary, who should ideally work together to meet the needs of society.

- There are three categories of care providers:

  - Public sector, where the majority of funding comes from local or national government. Recent changes in hospital status and so on make the division between public and private sector less clear.
  - Private sector, where funding comes from profits.
  - Voluntary sector, which are non-profit making organisations funded by voluntary contributions. Such agencies may have charitable status.

- There are two further divisions of care providers:

  - Statutory agencies have to provide their services by law, which also usually lays down minimum standards. The National Health Service, the DHSS and social services departments are all statutory providers.
  - Non-statutory agencies encompass the care providers who aren't part of the DHSS, NHS or SSD. This would include voluntary, commercial and informal agencies.

- The Welfare State was introduced to provide minimum standards of health, income, housing and education for the population. More recently there has been a difference of opinion over what constitutes minimum standards.

- The SSDs have changed over the years as a result of various government-sponsored reports and Acts. Their role is one of enablement within the community.

- Community care seeks to involve family, friends, the voluntary sector and also the private sector.

- SSDs are now more accountable in terms of what they do and how they spend their money.

- The term community care can be interpreted in two different ways:

  - care provided by the community for those in need
  - care provided by the caring services to help the needy stay within the community rather than admit them to institutions.

- Critics of the way community care is being provided say that it is being used as a cost-cutting exercise. Proponents say that it helps the individual to maintain self-respect and independence.

- Much of the work carried out in the SSD is carried out, or at least co-ordinated, by social workers. These social workers work on a 'patch' within the community or are attached to a residential centre.

  Generic social workers are trained to deal with all aspects of need; some may also specialise in a particular field of work.

- SSD customers are called clients. The process of referral is made either by the client, health service personnel, family, friends or neighbours.

- A social worker will make an initial visit to the client and assess their short- and long-term needs. This assessment will then be referred on to a specialist social worker in the patch team.

- The SSD has various services which can help the client maintain independent living. These services may give practical or financial help, or simply provide social contact.

- It will be necessary in many cases for the SSD to liaise with health service personnel to provide exactly what the client needs.

- SSDs have a statutory responsibility to provide residential care, known as Part 111 accommodation, for the elderly who can no longer look after themselves.

Assignment 6 The social services

TASK 1:
THE WELFARE
STATE

Find out about the four main Acts which created the Welfare State:

- The Education Act 1944
- The National Health Service Act 1946
- The National Assistance Act 1946
- The Children's Act 1948

Look at what provision there was before these Acts were introduced.

TASK 2:
FUNDING

All care provision needs to be funded some way or another. For the three types of provision:

- public
- private
- voluntary

look at where their funding comes from and how they allocate money.

TASK 3:
THE STATUTORY
SERVICES

Look at the following three statutory services:

- National Health Service
- Department of Health and Social Security
- Social Services Department

For each find out:

- where their funding comes from
- their defined roles and functions
- how they allocate funding
- recent changes in the way they are run.

TASK 4:
VOLUNTARY
AGENCIES

Find three national voluntary agencies that work for the elderly. For each, find out:

- how they raise money
- the work they do
- the number of paid staff and their roles
- the number of unpaid staff and their roles.

TASK 5:
LOCAL VOLUNTARY
ORGANISATIONS

Find out whether there are any local voluntary organisations in your area that work for the elderly and, if so, find out what they do and how they are funded.

TASK 6:
ACTS AND
GOVERNMENT
REPORTS

Look in more detail at the various reports and government Acts that have changed the way the SSDs work. The main reports are:

- The Seebohm Report 1968
- The Social Services Act 1970
- The Barclay Report 1982

TASK 7:
THE SOCIAL
WORKER'S ROLE

Look at the way the SSD in your area works for the needs of the elderly. You can ask to visit the department and/or invite a social worker to talk to your group.

Before meeting the social worker, decide what questions you would like to ask. Here are some areas you might like to find out more about:

- the increased use of private residential care for the elderly
- the effects of the Code of Practice called Home Life (Centre for Policy on Ageing 1984)
- your local authority's ethos on caring for the elderly, i.e. what importance they place in encouraging independence, etc.
- how much emphasis is placed on training care assistants
- what priority domiciliary care takes
- whether there are social workers with a special interest in the elderly.

Find out what daytime provision there is to cater for the elderly at home to help alleviate loneliness, financial problems, loss of mobility and so on.

When you have found out, arrange to make visits to find out more about them.

TASK 8:
COMMUNITY CARE

As a group discuss the advantages and disadvantages of community care. Decide on a conclusion – is community care for the good of the client or, ultimately, to save money?

7 The caring services 2 – The National Health Service

The National Health Service was set up in response to the National Health Service Act 1946. The Act aimed to provide a comprehensive health service, free of charge, to the whole population.

Before this, health care had been piecemeal with the rich able to pay for their treatment and the poor going without. The war had brought these disparities to people's attention. Many men were too unhealthy to join up as a result of poverty; the middle classes were shocked at the levels of malnutrition and poverty of many evacuees. The introduction of rationing, subsidised school meals and milk and child vaccination programmes improved the health of the nation and created the right conditions for change in health care provision.

The majority of the population had come to realise that the pre-war era of high unemployment could not continue; the blitz had destroyed many of the slums and given planners the opportunity to rebuild homes; and nationalisation and increased government control, were generally accepted. The time was right for the implementation of a free health service.

The National Health Service provision developed as a result of chance rather than planning. This was the reason given, ostensibly, by the Conservative government for introducing new health service initiatives in the 1980s and 1990s. As a result, the health service is undergoing a period of change; the divide between private and public sector health care is diminishing. NHS hospitals are forming self-governing trusts and private hospitals are providing opportunities for national staff training schemes. The profit motive has become a priority, which many say is a bad thing for a public service as staff tend to become disposable commodities in such circumstances.

The role of the NHS, rather like that of the Social Services, has become a political issue and is no longer an unchanging institution; it, too, has become the victim of market forces.

The role of the NHS

The NHS restructuring has involved many changes. The overall intention was to give more autonomy to the various providers of health care. Hospitals can now 'opt out' to become self-governing trusts, so will, in

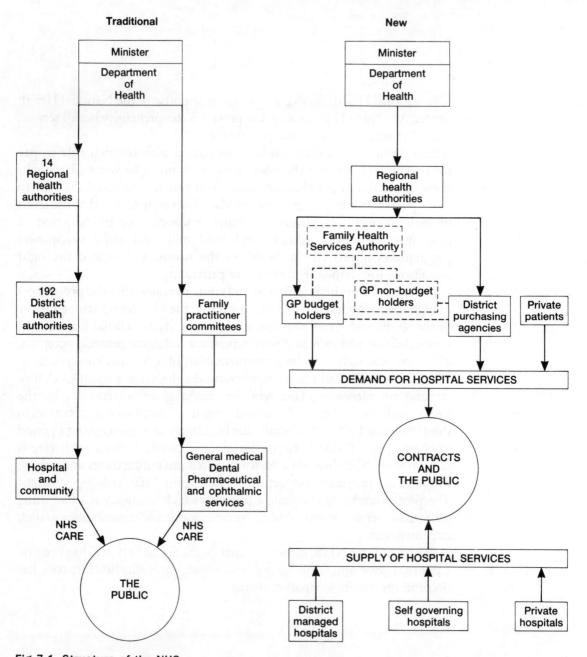

Fig 7.1 Structure of the NHS

Whole time equivalent (WTE)

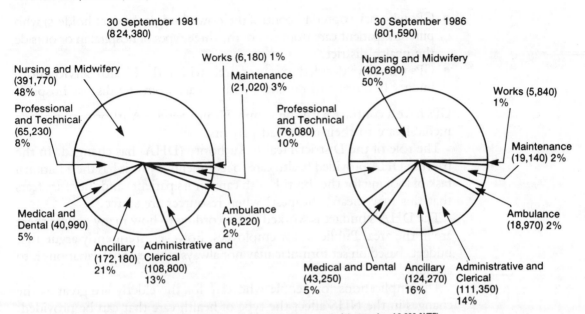

30 September 1981
(824,380)

Works (6,180) 1%

Maintenance
(21,020) 3%

Nursing and Midwifery
(391,770)
48%

Professional
and Technical
(65,230)
8%

Medical and
Dental (40,990)
5%

Ancillary
(172,180)
21%

Administrative and
Clerical
(108,800)
13%

Ambulance
(18,220)
2%

30 September 1986
(801,590)

Nursing and Midwifery
(402,690)
50%

Works (5,840)
1%

Professional
and Technical
(76,080)
10%

Maintenance
(19,140) 2%

Ambulance
(18,970) 2%

Medical and Dental
(43,250)
5%

Ancillary
(124,270)
16%

Administrative and
Clerical
(111,350)
14%

NOTE: 1. The figures used to compile this graph have not been adjusted to take account of the transfer of 2,600 (WTE)
Operating Department Assistants from Ancillary to Professional and Technical Staff on 1 April 1984.

2. Figures (WTES) have been independently rounded to the nearest 10. Percentages have
been rounded to the nearest whole number.

Fig 7.2 NHS Directly Employed Staff: Comparison of main staff groups (England) 1981–1986
(Taken from *The Health Service in England Annual Report 1989*. Reproduced by kind permission of HMSO. Crown copyright 1990)

effect, sell their services. General practitioners (GPs) now have the option
to control their own budgets and can buy treatment from the hospitals;
GPs who wish to stay as they were can still refer patients to the local
hospital.

The District Health Authorities are allocated funding based on the
number and age of the people in the area. This money is used to buy health
care which means that health care providers, mainly hospitals, have to
compete for trade.

This 'market-place' approach is seen by many to be ultimately doomed
to failure as funding in real terms has been reduced over the years. These
critics argue that patients are not the same as customers and the services
provided by hospitals etc. cannot really be measured in terms of profit.
There is the very real danger that, in order to save money, patients will
be referred to the *cheapest* provider rather than the *best*. Those in favour
of such a system stress that it offers more freedom for the hospital to provide
the services the population needs and to improve patient care.

Under the new system, there are three types of hospital care available:

● district hospitals
● self-governing hospitals (those that have 'opted out')
● private hospitals.

Similarly, there are two types of General Practitioner services available:

- GPs who have opted to control their own budget (budget holders) who purchase patient care from any of the three types of hospital in or outside the health district.
- GPs who have decided to stay entirely within the Health Service (non-budget holders) and purchase patient care from the district hospital.

GPs have a contract with the Family Health Service Authority to provide medical care to their registered patients.

The role of the District Health Authority (DHA) has changed. In the past the DHA provided health care to its patients. Now it has the additional task of looking for the 'best' health care for its patients and there are fears that this may mean 'cheapest' when resources are scarce.

The DHA's budget is worked out according to how many people there are in the area. Public sector employees, however, frequently argue that budgets based on set formulae may not always take regional variations into account.

The implications for people who care for the elderly are great as the changes in the NHS affect the type of health care that can be provided. Awareness of this issue is apparent in the new training initiatives for carers and nurses.

The NHS and the elderly

This section will examine NHS provision for the elderly. Private provision will be expanded in the assignment section and in Chapter 9.

Health care is usually divided into two sections, but there can be three:

- **primary health care** is the term for health care in the community. It is usual to find the staff of the primary health care team in either a health centre or GP practice.
- **secondary health care** is care provided by the staff in hospital. The elderly may be treated as either outpatients or as inpatients. The hospital can also provide staff to visit patients in their homes as part of community care provision.
- **tertiary health care** is the care provided by long-term care institutions (*see* Chapter 9, long-term residential care).

The primary health care team

The primary health care team consists of one or more of the following:

- general practitioner
- community nurse
- practice nurse
- health visitor
- midwife.

These personnel make up the basis of the primary health care team. There are other personnel, however, who can be called upon to assist in patient care when the need arises:

- receptionist
- social worker
- counsellor
- chiropodist
- physiotherapist
- occupational therapist
- speech therapist.

Primary health care provision is the patient's first contact with the health service, unless they require emergency admission to hospital. It is therefore important that the GP's practice or health centre makes every attempt to make the elderly feel confident about coming to see them with their problems. Many elderly people feel reluctant to visit the GP for some of the following reasons:

- the development of group practices means that it isn't always possible to visit the same doctor.
- the larger premises make them feel lost and personal care isn't always possible.
- modern technology, with intercoms, lights and buzzers can be overwhelming.

Statistically, the elderly patient is more likely to need referral to a specialist, follow-up care and home visits, which makes a greater demand on resources. The GP's payments, however, recognise this additional demand.

It is not easy to separate the individual roles of each member of the team as they are closely interrelated by the need for regular liaison. It is, however, useful to know the general role of each member.

The role of the GP

The role of the doctor in general practice is:

- to diagnose and treat health disorders
- to give health checks and offer screening services
- to issue prescriptions if necessary
- to refer the patient on to other services
- to recommend the services of other members of the team
- to give advice where needed.

The GP also needs to be aware of other issues; the patient is an individual and may have needs additional to the health disorder. A good GP will develop counselling skills and a patient-centred approach. In addition, the GP's services need to be supported by motivated staff.

The receptionist

The receptionist has an important role in the health centre or GP's practice which is often overlooked. The elderly are frequently reluctant to visit the GP, often feeling that they are wasting the doctor's time. The receptionist's attitude can either reinforce this view or help to make the reluctant elderly feel confident. The receptionist may also be asked for advice, so needs to think very carefully before offering it.

The community nurse

The role of the community nurse is to offer patients nursing care in their own homes. Around half the community nurse's caseload is elderly patients who want to remain independent and in their own home for as long as possible.

The community nurse may be required to do any of the following nursing tasks:

- changing dressings
- giving injections and other medication
- giving bed baths
- checking blood pressure
- liaising with other health or social service personnel.

The community nurse offers direct nursing care to the elderly patient and will be aware, through regular visits, of any deterioration in the patient's condition.

The practice nurse

The practice nurse's role is to provide nursing care in the practice premises or health centre. This means that the GP's time can be freed to deal with other patients.

The health visitor

The health visitor has less contact with elderly patients. The health visitor's role is to work with the fit elderly and offer advice on health care issues. The majority of their caseload concerns families with young children.

Other members of the practice team

Some of the larger practices offer the services of the following personnel:

- a social worker to help and advise patients who can visit the premises. These social workers will be well-informed about the type of information needed by patients.
- a chiropodist to care for the feet. Men over 65 and women over 60 are entitled to free chiropody.
- a physiotherapist, occupational therapist and speech therapist who will offer care and treatment in the home.

The future

There is an increasing number of elderly people in the population and this fact needs to be accommodated in future plans for the Health Service. Primary health care of the elderly patient is frequently demanding as they often have more than one problem. It is demanding both in terms of human and financial resources, and this needs to be recognised by those who plan for the future. A pre-set formula does not always take these variations into account.

Secondary health care

The patient will visit the hospital either as an outpatient, following GP referral, or as an emergency admission.

As an outpatient, the patient may attend hospital for any of the following reasons:

- to see a specialist doctor, usually called a consultant, about a specific health disorder
- for health screening services such as X-Ray, blood and other testing facilities in the pathology laboratory
- to receive physiotherapy, occupational therapy or speech therapy.

As an emergency admission, depending on the nature of the disorder, the elderly patient could find themselves on any of the wards except those dealing with pregnancy, childbirth and children.

Changes in the NHS and its funding have not affected the variety of hospitals offering health care to the elderly patient:

- general hospitals serving a district which offer the complete range of services, including a care of the elderly unit
- psychiatric hospitals, catering for the mentally ill, usually have a high proportion of elderly patients
- private health provision which includes hospitals, clinics, GPs, nurses, eye and teeth treatment, chiropody and psychiatric help. The provision is the same as that provided by the NHS, but is paid for either directly by the patient or by private health insurance schemes
- hospices which care for the terminally ill
- day hospitals which, as the name suggests, provide care on a daily basis.

Care of the elderly units

Care of the elderly uses the highest proportion of the NHS services. A good care of the elderly unit will provide health care for all elderly patients, even those in other wards, and they will also offer outpatient and rehabilitation care. As the term geriatric has some bad associations, many hospitals have renamed the geriatric unit the care of the elderly unit.

The main aim of these units is to provide the following services:

- diagnosis
- treatment
- rehabilitation into the community
- aftercare.

As well as caring for the health needs of the elderly patient, the unit will take account of their social needs and provide activities and social contact. The day hospital can provide the same standard and variety of care. Patients usually attend a few days a week rather than daily.

It is becoming increasingly more common for people to die in hospital, so it has to be accepted that many patients in care of the elderly units will die there – the figure is around 30 per cent.

Elderly patients may be offered treatment by any of a variety of hospital staff.

The consultant is a specialist doctor who has ultimate responsibility for all the treatment the patient receives. The consultant oversees a team of doctors:

- the senior registrars, who deputise for the consultant
- registrars, who carry out operations
- senior house officers, who carry out operations under supervision and prescribe drugs
- house officers, who are newly-qualified doctors who either intend working in a hospital or becoming GPs. House officers have the most contact with patients and can prescribe drugs.

The nurse. There are two types of nurse, the Registered General Nurse, who gives more specialist treatment to the patient, and the Healthcare Assistant, who will deal with the more basic nursing tasks. Some nurses specialise in care of the elderly.

The occuptional therapist uses leisure and occupational activities to treat physical and mental illnesses. Stroke patients frequently need the occupational therapist to help them regain some independence.

The physiotherapist uses activities and exercises to:

- treat diseases of the bones, joints and muscles
- prevent the disorder from getting worse
- treat injuries to the bones, joints and muscles and rehabilitate the patient
- maintain mobility to enable maximum independence.

The speech therapist helps people with disorders of the voice, speech or language resulting from injury or disease. Speech is often affected by a stroke.

Psychologists look at how people react and adapt to various situations. They will see patients suffering from phobias, depression, stress, anxiety states and other disorders that prevent them from functioning normally. In the care of the elderly unit they may be involved in designing suitable living conditions and rehabilitating them into the community.

Psychiatrists are trained doctors who have specialised in psychiatry. They may work in the community, in a psychiatric hospital or day centre, or specialise in specific patient groups such as the elderly.

The psychiatrist will look at mental disorders such as:

- mental illness, e.g. confusional states, dementia, schizophrenia, depression
- mental disorders resulting from drug abuse, including alcohol.

The larger hospitals will often employ the services of a **hospital social worker**, previously known as an almoner, who offers advice on financial problems, domiciliary care, aids and adaptations in the home and follow-up support following discharge.

Anaesthetists are doctors specialising in the area of anaesthetics. The elderly patient will meet the anaesthetist before and after an operation.

The radiographer takes X-Rays and computer scans to detect illness and injury.

The pathology laboratory staff look at various samples to detect illness. Illnesses can be detected by examining blood, sputum, urine, stools, etc.

The dietician will look at special diets needed by patients. This may be required because of illness, allergy or obesity.

There are many other people working in a hospital who are vital to the smooth running of the service. These include the porters, voluntary helpers, canteen staff, administration staff and maintenance staff.

Liaison

The health needs of the elderly person are diverse and any provision needs to take this diversity into account. Over the years there has been much valuable research into care of the elderly. The overall conclusion seems to be that a comprehensive network of care provision is needed with liaison between *all* carers – from public, private and voluntary sectors, health and social services and the community.

This approach works well on the 'patch' system used in community provision. It allows for joint planning, implementation, modification and feedback. With reduced funding it is vital that all personnel involved collaborate and co-ordinate their provision to ensure the best possible service for the patient or client.

Key issues – a summary

- The National Health Service (NHS) was set up to provide a free health service to the population to ensure minimum standards of health.

- As a result of government initiatives in the 1980s and 1990s, the NHS has undergone changes to make it respond to market forces.

- The restructuring is intended to bring about more autonomy to health care providers.

- Hospitals may 'opt out' of the NHS.

- General Practitioners (GPs) have the option of becoming budget-holders.

- District Health Authorities (DHAs) are allocated a budget based on the number and age of the local population.

- Critics of the 'market led' approach to health care provision say that patients are not the same as customers and health care provision is not the same as a product; it has no real profit potential.

- Advocates of the restructured system say it offers freedom to the health care providers which will improve services.

- Primary health care provision is that provided by a GP practice or health centre. It is usually the patient's first contact point with the NHS.

- Secondary health care is the services provided by the hospital.

- Tertiary health care is the care provided by residential institutions.

- Primary and secondary health care teams are closely linked as they need to liaise over patient care, with some staff working in both a hospital and the community.

- The aim of primary and secondary health care staff is to maintain the elderly patient's independence for as long as possible by providing community care.

- The care of the elderly unit aims to provide a high standard of specialist care for the elderly. Many of these specialists will see the patient following discharge from hospital.

- Good practice in health care for the elderly is to see the patient as central to provision.

- Good liaison between the services is vital.

Assignment 7 The National Health Service

TASK 1: PRE-NHS HEALTH CARE	Look up health care provision before the introduction of the NHS. Look at:

- types of provision
- standard of provision

- training of staff
- funding and costs.

TASK 2:
THE NHS ACT 1946
Look up the National Health Service Act of 1946 and consider its aims and the way it was to be implemented.

TASK 3:
RESTRUCTURING OF THE NHS
The Conservative Government introduced a number of changes into the NHS in the 1980s and 1990s. Look at the following factors:

- what the changes were
- why the changes were introduced
- who was affected by the changes
- self-governing trusts for hospitals
- budget-holder GPs
- the advantages and disadvantages of the restructured system
- the role of the private sector
- the role of the District Health Authority.

TASK 4:
NHS'S ETHOS
As a group, discuss whether health care provision should be governed by market forces.

TASK 5:
GP PRACTICE AUDIT
Visit a local GP practice or health centre and carry out an audit of their provision. You may find these ideas helpful starting points.

- The premises:
  —age
  —size
  —layout
  —equipment.
- Staffing:
  —number of staff, full and part-time
  —type of job, i.e. GP, district nurse, health visitor, etc.
- Care provision:
  —variety of service available
  —when they are available
  —community care provision
  —liaison with other services.
- Patients:
  —number of patients on register
  —number of patients according to age, sex, etc.
  —geographical catchment area.

When you have collected this information, put it together as an information pack.

TASK 6:
PRIMARY CARE FOR THE ELDERLY
While you are visiting the practice or health centre, arrange to interview a member of staff to find out the following:

- the steps that have been taken to make the centre available to the elderly patient.

- how the receptionists are trained to deal with patients in general and the elderly in particular.
- how the community nurse provides care for the elderly patients in their own homes.
- the type of nursing the practice nurse will provide for elderly patients.
- whether there are links with other agencies.

TASK 7:
EVALUATION

When you have completed your work on primary health care provision hold a group discussion to evaluate the following:

- whether the provision is satisfactory
- what changes, if any, need to be made
- whether staff are satisfied
- whether patient needs are met adequately
- ideas for the future.

TASK 8:
SECONDARY HEALTH
CARE

Arrange to either visit your local hospital, or ask a member of staff to visit you, in order to carry out some research. Some of the following headings may help you to plan your work.

- premises:
  - —position
  - —accessibility
  - —size
  - —age
  - —design
  - —geographical area covered.
- provision:
  - —whether a teaching hospital
  - —disorders dealt with, i.e. the wards available, whether there is a casualty department, etc.
  - —health-screening services
  - —research provision
  - —whether there is a care of the elderly unit.
- funding:
  - —whether it is funded by a trust or the DHA
  - —income-generating schemes, if any.
- opinions:
  - —talk to staff to find out their views on the standard of health care provided for patients in general and the elderly in particular.

TASK 9:
THE CARE OF THE
ELDERLY UNIT

Arrange a visit to the care of the elderly unit to look into provision using these headings:

- health care available
- number and type of patient

- whether confused or mentally ill patients are catered for
- whether there is a day-care facility
- activities provided
- number of staff, i.e. patient:staff ratio
- staff opinions of provision.

When you have collected this information, use it as the basis for a series of recommendations on good practice in care of the elderly units.

TASK 10:
THE SECONDARY
HEALTH CARE TEAM

If you feel you need to know more about the role of the various staff in a hospital then find out, either from the staff themselves or by research.

Members of the secondary health care team include:

- consultant
- senior registrar
- registrar
- senior house officers
- house officers
- registered general nurse
- healthcare assistant
- occupational therapist
- physiotherapist
- speech therapist
- psychologist
- psychiatrist
- hospital social worker
- anaesthetist
- radiographer
- pathology laboratory staff
- dietician
- voluntary helpers.

TASK 11:
ELDERLY CARE –
AN OVERVIEW

You have looked at the role of the social services and the health services and are now in a position to make some comments.

As a group, evaluate the provision of the two services and make recommendations for improvement in provision. You may wish to separate your ideas into the following areas:

- staff job satisfaction
- patient satisfaction
- financial aspects
- government intervention
- training needs.

8

The caring services 3 – The voluntary and private sectors

Voluntary sector care provision is that which is not provided on a statutory or profit-making basis. It is run by charitable and other non-profit making organisations, and is independent of the state. Private sector care, however, is profit-motivated so cannot register as a charity.

Voluntary sector care provision

To become a charity, an organisation has to satisfy the Charity Commission that it is providing for the needs of society, perhaps through religious, educational or financial means, and does not have a political bias. Once the organisation becomes a registered charity it is eligible for tax relief and other monetary support. Just under half the voluntary sector organisations have charitable status.

It is wrong to assume that all voluntary organisations employ unpaid staff. Although some may use unpaid volunteer staff, others may have only salaried staff. Most organisations use a combination of paid and unpaid staff. It has been found that, in the long term, it pays to employ some staff at the full market rate for a number of reasons:

- the status of the organisation is raised in the eyes of both the staff and the public
- a member of staff with, say, fund-raising experience, could cover the costs of his or her salary and more by increasing funds
- salaried staff offer stability in terms of length of service which is important in, for instance, administrative areas of work where continuity is vital, or in posts needing specific training.

Like many of today's institutions, voluntary organisations developed as a result of specific needs in the nineteenth century, so had no overall cohesion and grew into a mish-mash of provision. Many were started by philanthropic rich people or by religious establishments. More recently, the voluntary sector has developed into certain clear areas of provision:

- organisations set up to deal with a one-off, specific need
- organisations dealing with a specific client group, e.g. Age Concern, CRUSE
- organisations concerned with a particular health problem, e.g. Parkinson's Disease Society, Alcoholics Anonymous, Alzheimer's Disease Society
- organisations aiming to educate and pressure groups, e.g. Action on Smoking and Health, Voluntary Euthanasia Society
- organisations may be national or local, depending on their overall aims and intentions.

These areas are not mutually exclusive, and there is an overlap both between voluntary agencies and with the statutory sector providers which is becoming increasingly important.

The links between the voluntary and statutory sectors

The links between voluntary and statutory sector care providers is complex. Ideally, both sectors should be offering a complementary service rather than competing with each other. What each can offer may not suit all clients, and the two sectors offer freedom of choice. Close liaison is important as information and experience can be shared, pooling research resources and avoiding 're-invention of the wheel' situations.

Some clients express a preference for the type of care and support they require. Those preferring to approach the voluntary sector first give the following reasons:

- there is concern expressed about being put 'on record' by the NHS or SSD staff
- there is a feeling of having failed if they are seeking professional help
- there is a sense of losing personal identity when being the subject of a social worker's case load
- many people feel alienated by professionals which creates a communication barrier
- there is a reluctance to allow professionals to 'take over' their problem because of the sense of losing independence.

Although client choice is important, it is sometimes necessary for the statutory services to be involved. Modern caring professionals are more aware of good practice in dealing with clients, so many of the fears expressed above will be dispelled.

In the 1980s and 1990s the Conservative Government placed great emphasis on encouraging the growth of voluntary sector care provision.

The argument was that the voluntary sector was a large area of untapped enthusiasm and resources which should be implemented to work in association with the statutory sector to offer a wider client choice. The opposing view argues that the Welfare State guarantees minimum standards of care for the population and it has to be asked, therefore, whether it is right that the statutory services should regard voluntary sector provision as an integral part of care provision in the community rather than the 'icing on the cake'. It is felt that the statutory services are now relying on the voluntary sector to such an extent that their removal would detrimentally affect statutory provision. The case goes on to suggest that such reliance is potentially dangerous and is motivated by a desire to cut costs rather than by a consideration of client needs.

The greatest advantages of voluntary agencies come from their flexibility – they can respond to changing needs more quickly than the statutory agencies as they are governed by fewer rules and regulations. This spontaneity means that they are often at the forefront in roles that require:

- giving advice
- fighting to change public and state opinion
- speaking on behalf of individuals or groups.

For this reason they are a very useful support to the work done by the statutory sector. They also offer volunteer staff the opportunity for self-development through their work.

The private sector

The main aim of private sector provision is to run each organisation on a profit-making basis. This does not mean that private sector care provision is a bad thing, but any client does need to either be able to pay for their care or to have their care paid for. This clearly removes schemes that are unlikely to generate profits and clients demanding more intensive care from the private agenda.

Private sector care can operate on various levels:

- hospitals can be an entirely commercial enterprise, with both staff and premises working entirely in the private sector
- NHS facilities, including premises, staff and equipment, can be used for private health patients
- parts of state sector work, such as the canteen or laundry, are put out to private tender
- NHS staff can do some work in the private sector
- some SSD work may be put out to private tender, such as home help provision
- many residential homes for the elderly are in the private sector.

It is argued that private sector care provision broadens client choice and improves client care by introducing the element of competition. However, if making money is the prime motive then unprofitable services may either disappear or be left solely to the statutory services. This would then create a two-tier system; one tier for the rich and one for the poor. In this kind of situation the fear is that the only client group with a truly improved choice and standard of care will be the group who can afford to pay for it.

Key points – a summary

- Voluntary sector care provision is independent of the state and the profit motive.

- Private sector care provision provides care but has the overall aim of making money.

- Most voluntary agencies employ paid staff in key roles to raise status and give continuity.

- The voluntary sector can offer a wide range of provision as each agency has different aims and objectives. They may be local or national.

- It is important to be clear about the different roles of the statutory and voluntary sector.

- The voluntary agencies need to maintain their independence and avoid becoming an adjunct of the statutory sector.

- Because of their relative freedom from rules and regulations the voluntary sector can respond more quickly to changing needs.

- Private sector care provision, because of its need to make a profit, will always leave gaps in care provision. There are some client groups who are unlikely to generate profits.

- Private care provision can also operate within statutory agencies.

Assignment 8 Non-statutory caring services

TASK 1:
WHAT ARE
VOLUNTARY
AGENCIES?

The voluntary sector is made up of a number of different agencies offering a wide variety of provision. Find out more about the meaning of the term 'voluntary agencies'. You may wish to include:

- the role of the Charity Commission
- a definition of the term voluntary
- a historical background.

TASK 2:
HOW DO THEY
OPERATE?

Choose one voluntary sector agency from each of these four areas who may provide help or care for the elderly:

- an organisation set up to deal with a one-off need. This can be either local or national
- an organisation dealing specifically with the elderly
- an organisation dealing with a particular health problem that may affect the elderly
- a pressure group or group seeking to educate.

When you have chosen your agencies, look at them in some detail and make an evaluation. The following ideas may help you to group your thoughts:

- the overall aim of the agency
- the motivating factor of each agency, i.e. whether religious, educational, etc.
- availability and accessibility of the agency
- how funds are raised
- staffing patterns, i.e. whether paid employees or unpaid volunteers
- how the provision is delivered
- whether the agency has used advertising campaigns and, if so, an evaluation of success
- whether the agency's provision parallels or adds to that of the statutory sector.

Use this information to compile a factsheet on the four agencies.

When you have completed the factsheet, as a group evaluate the overall success of each agency and draw any relevant conclusions.

TASK 3:
LOCAL LIAISON

Look at the relationship between the statutory and voluntary sector care provision in your area. To do this you will need to contact key personnel in the three areas of health care, social care and voluntary care providers.

The general areas you will need to look at are:

- provision
- degree of overlap in provision
- patterns of liaison between the agencies
- any comments or criticisms of the present system operating in the area
- whether the system improves client choice.

TASK 4:
VOLUNTARY SECTOR
WORKERS

Arrange to speak with a voluntary sector worker, either paid or unpaid, to find out about:

- their role
- what motivated them to work for the agency

- their comments on the agency's work
- their comments on the clients
- how they regard working in the voluntary sector.

TASK 5:
THE ETHICAL
DEBATE

In the light of the information you have found out about the relationship between voluntary and statutory sector care provision, discuss these two comments:

'The voluntary agencies provide an untapped wealth of human resources whcih should be encouraged to work alongside the statutory providers in order to provide maximum choice fo the client.'

'It is typical of politicans to use the voluntary agencies so they can cut funding to the statutory care providing agencies.'

TASK 6:
A PRIVATE
RESIDENTIAL HOME

Arrange to visit a privately-run residential home for the elderly in your area so you can make a comparison between public and private provision.

You should prepare a set of questions before your visit; the following suggestions may be helpful:

- the premises:
  —age
  —size
  —plan of layout.
- accommodation:
  —number of bedrooms
  —whether shared or single rooms
  —bathroom facilities, i.e. whether shared, en-suite, etc.
  —catering facilities, i.e. whether there is the opportunity for
    self-catering
  —whether there is access to the grounds
  —whether there is a communal lounge
  —type of furniture.
- facilities:
  —whether a lift is installed
  —any aids and adaptations installed
  —leisure facilities
  —whether there is a unit for the confused.
- staffing:
  —number of staff, full and part-time
  —staff: resident ratio
  —degree and level of staff training.
- routines:
  —whether mealtimes are flexible
  —what the visiting arrangements are

—how arrangements are made for hairdressing, chiropody, dental treatment, etc.

—how admissions are made

—the basis for charges, i.e. do all residents pay the same? Does the SSD pay for some?

Using the answers to these questions, and any others you may have asked, write about the home. How do you feel it compares with a public sector residential home?

TASK 7:
THE CARE DEBATE
– PUBLIC VS.
PRIVATE

There are some elderly clients, such as those with Alzheimer's Disease, who will need continuous and person-intensive care. It is, therefore, unlikely that the private sector will be able to cope with their needs as the amount of care they demand will reduce profits.

Some people believe that clients like this may be left to the reduced provision of the public sector while the private sector cares only for the more able clients, thus creating a two-tier system.

As a group, discuss how likely this is to happen.

9 Care of the elderly – a co-ordinated response

It is not the responsibility of any one person or group of people to ensure that the elderly receive a high standard of care. In a caring society, such as ours is considered to be, every individual member of society has a responsibility for caring. Every day we can see examples of caring:

- neighbours keeping an eye on an elderly person next door
- supporting voluntary agencies with money
- giving time to voluntary agencies
- lobbying local and county councils and government bodies about important issues
- working with the elderly.

Some of this help is spontaneous and some is part of care provision, and both are important. Statutory and voluntary provision both rely on friends and neighbours to report any problems.

Levels of need

The caring needs of the elderly range from needing no more help than the average person in society to needing complete nursing care, 24 hours a day. One of the problems for the professional caring services is to assess these needs accurately, balancing independence with health and safety.

Such decisions are made in consultation with the individual concerned, as far as possible, and their family. It is, nevertheless, a serious responsibility for the caring services.

Level 1 – self care

The majority of the elderly live independent lives at home, calling on the health and social services if their help is needed. They are able to make decisions about their needs and demand very little outside help. Family, friends and neighbours may be there if needed, but are not an integral part of their caring needs.

Level 2 –
informal care
provision

The next category are the elderly who are, in the main, quite capable of looking after themselves, but need some help from the health and/or social services.

Some examples of the type of support they may need include:

- An elderly couple need extra help. He is recovering from a stroke and she has high blood pressure and a weak heart. The help provided is:
  —a home help twice a week to shop and clean
  —the district nurse to give medical care and to bath the husband
  —occupational therapy for the husband.
- An elderly person has leg ulcers that need dressing daily. She cannot get to the GP's surgery so the district nurse comes to her house each morning to change the dressings.
- An elderly man who is reasonably fit but finds it increasingly difficult to cook for himself is brought meals-on-wheels every day. The cost of the meals is subsidised by the council, so he is charged a reduced fee.

Level 3 –
community care

Community care offers this type of domiciliary support, the overall aim of which is for the elderly to maintain independence for as long as possible (*see* Chapter 6 p 92). The people involved in decisions about community care provision are:

- the client
- the professional caring services:
  —the Health Service
  —the social services
- the voluntary sector
- the private sector
- family
- friends
- neighbours.

All these people may play a part in providing care for the elderly.

Level 4 –
increased
support

The next level of care is when the client needs more support than simply visits from the caring services. Their mental or physical health may have deteriorated to such an extent that they are either a potential danger to themselves, or their friends and family can no longer cope all the time. They may not need full-time care, so will be offered day care, either in a day-care centre or in a hospital care of the elderly unit. The centre will offer activities and general personal and medical care.

When the elderly couple or person is no longer safe to be left alone, or feels ready to move on from their own home, there may be the option of going into sheltered accommodation. Sheltered accommodation is flats or bed-sitting rooms, generally on one site, where a warden is in attendance who can offer help when needed.

Level 5 – long-term residential care

The final level of care is when the client needs full-time care, either in a residential home or in a hospital. This decision is never taken lightly; all the factors will have been carefully considered by the parties involved. Residential care is called Part 111 accommodation.

To understand the wide variety of types, levels and standards of care available for the elderly, the next three sections will examine the main areas of care provision:

- Community Care – support from the community
- sheltered accommodation – including care from the community
- long-term residential care.

Community care – factors affecting provision

Chapters 6, 7 and 8 discussed the contributions of the various caring services to overall community care provision through the domiciliary support they offer. These services are usually co-ordinated by the social services as the social work patch team will be aware of the differing types of care provision available in the area, and will therefore be able to offer the client informed advice. There are various factors that affect the standard of care provision available.

- Community care provision is undermined by any cuts in public expenditure. Financial cuts generally reduce services such as meals-on-wheels, home helps, day centres, home visits from, for example, chiropodists, etc.
- The standards of community care provision are variable, with the inner city areas generally providing a good level of provision and the rural areas less so.
- Areas will vary in how they assess needs. For example, some areas will provide a weekly home help service to the elderly whereas others will only provide a home help if the client is very frail and in a poor state of health.
- Because of improved health care and diet, people are living longer, and poor health tends to develop later than in the past. The average age of residents in care of the elderly homes has increased to 85 years, which means that community care providers will need to cater for an increasing number of elderly clients.

Community care provision – an overview

The types of domiciliary care provided by the SSDs were outlined in Chapter 6. The provision varies from area to area, so an awareness of these variations would be useful to people working in the care sector.

The Health Service, in conjunction with the SSD, provides medical domiciliary care, according to individual need (*see* Chapter 7).

The voluntary sector makes an increasingly vital contribution to care provision, offering additional choice and often compensating for inadequate public sector provision.

The private sector provides care either to those who can afford it or to the local authority.

Day centres, which may be run by the public or the voluntary sector, are an important part of community care provision. The Centre for Policy on Ageing states that there are 39,000 SSD day centre places available for the elderly and a further 12,000 places in voluntary sector centres. Although not all these places are available every day, the spaces that are are not always taken up. Rural area take-up is lower than that of urban areas, possibly because of transport difficulties and the distances involved.

	Number of dwellings			
	1981	1986	1988	1989
Sheltered housing				
Private enterprise	130	850	2,195	3,289
Housing associations	1,929	1,916	1,631	1,101
Local authorities/new towns	5,558	3,722	2,820	2,590
Other housing				
Private enterprise	62	193	578	552
Housing associations	261	597	345	344
Local authorities/new towns	4,636	1,778	1,377	992
All dwellings for the elderly	12,576	9,056	8,946	8,868

Fig 9.1 Completions of new specialised dwellings for the elderly: by sector (England)

(*Source*: Department of the Environment. Reproduced by kind permission of HMSO. Crown copyright)

The cost of day care to the client also varies greatly from area to area, with some SSDs charging for the day centre places while others are either subsidising the costs or providing a free service. The implications of introducing charges are twofold:

● The clients may feel they have more of a voice about the running of the centre if they are contributing towards costs.

- Variations within areas such as charging for places in day centres for the elderly but not for the handicapped, or between areas, could create an unfair and arbitrary system.

Sheltered accommodation – factors affecting provision

Sheltered accommodation, which can be provided by the public, private or voluntary sectors, bridges the gap between the elderly living in their own home and moving on to Part 111 accommodation.

The idea behind sheltered accommodation, which originated in the 1950s, was to enable the elderly to live independent lives with support if needed. They would have their own possessions in a bed-sitting room, but share kitchen and bathroom facilities. Modern sheltered accommodation now reflects both the higher demands of society (*see* Fig 9.1) and demographic changes:

- People are no longer happy to share facilities, so many public sector sheltered accommodation buildings are redundant. The private sector has built self-contained accommodation, but this is more suitable to the more active elderly as there is little other provision available.
- Local authorities are working in conjunction with housing associations to provide suitable accommodation at realistic prices, both for the individual and for the authority.
- There is an increasing number of older and frailer people who will need some sort of appropriate housing.
- People are demanding a greater say in their own destiny; owner-occupation, which has been greatly encouraged since the 1970s, will probably be transferred to sheltered accommodation premises.
- As a result of the shift towards independence, people are more reluctant to move into Part 111 accommodation until it is absolutely necessary.
- Various government initiatives, the Griffiths Report 1988, the White Paper 1989 and the Act 1990, have the following implications:
  —Local authorities change from becoming the providers of services for the elderly, which included provision of accommodation, to purchasers of services from the private and voluntary sector.
  —Local authorities have overall responsibility for care provision, but should intervene as little as possible, leaving it to the effects of market forces.
  —Local authorities have to make their planning strategies available and use private and voluntary organisations in addition to public sector services.

Although these initiatives may not all be implemented, they do point the way to future developments.

Sheltered accommodation – an overview

Public sector sheltered accommodation can be divided into two types of provision:

- extra sheltered housing
- sheltered housing with care.

The private sector parallels this by providing:

- close care facilities
- continuing care villages.

It is planned that this provision will be suitable for the elderly either until they need hospitalisation or die.

The accommodation provided in extra sheltered housing and continuing care village units is usually self-contained flats or flatlets which may provide any of the following facilities:

- a communal dining room that provides at least one meal a day
- assisted bathing
- medical facilities to be used by domiciliary health care professionals such as a visiting GP, district nurse, physiotherapist, etc.

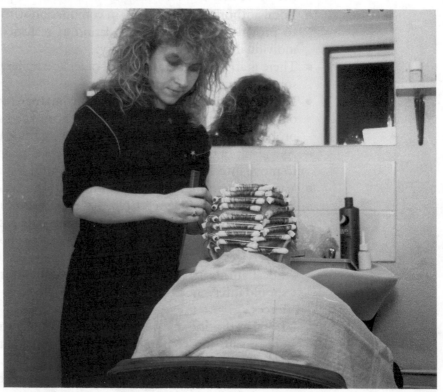

© Emma Flack

© Emma Flack

- care provision such as hairdressing, chiropody, exercising, etc.
- shopping facilities
- laundry facilities
- activities such as handicrafts and art
- day-care centre to meet other people
- facilities to entertain visitors.

There are criticisms of attempts to provide a range of continuing care provision on one site:

- the younger elderly may be unwilling to be confronted by visions of the old elderly as it may be a reminder of what could be in store for them
- the private insurance costs needed to pay for the care provided would be too high for many people.

The private sector have, in the past, made some errors of judgement in designing sheltered accommodation. Mistakes include:

- building the accommodation on more than one storey without installing lifts
- not incorporating ramps and wider doorways into design.

Such lack of planning meant that the elderly would have to move when their condition deteriorated.

More recently, however, the private sector has become aware of the need for careful design. Unfortunately, the elderly most likely to benefit are the well-off as the majority of private provision caters for the rich minority of the elderly living, on the whole, in the Home Counties.

The next step is to encourage the private sector to provide sheltered accommodation for a wider segment of the elderly population. This implies a need to consider both alternative methods of funding and long-term planning. Some thoughts for the future could be:

- With the increase in owner-occupiers in housing generally, the elderly of the future may be able to use the value of their house as collateral.
- Insurance companies could develop schemes that enable younger people to insure themselves for long-term care.

Long-term sheltered residential care

This is the next stage in accommodation and support, and is suitable for the older elderly needing more care and support but who may still retain a degree of independence. This provision is found in the sheltered housing with care schemes which may offer the following facilities:

- groups of residents living in self-contained units around a central living/dining room
- food provided by either a central kitchen or on-site kitchen and eaten in the unit or dining room
- 24-hour cover in order to respond to possible emergencies

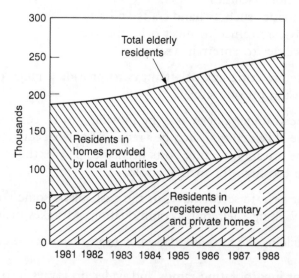

Residents aged 65 and over in homes for elderly people and homes for the younger physically handicapped. Figures for Wales also include residents in homes for the blind.

Fig 9.2 Elderly people in residential accommodation[1] (United Kingdom)

(*Source*: Department of Health; Social Work Services Group, Scottish Office; Welsh Office; Department of Health, Northern Ireland. Reproduced by kind permission of HMSO. Crown copyright)

- staff accommodation
- provision of respite care facilities for the elderly being cared for by relatives.

Such schemes aim to offer flexibility and try to avoid the sense of institutionalisation.

However, there are elderly people who need extra care in accommodation provided by public, private and voluntary sector organisations – residential home care.

Residential home care

The reasons for going into a residential home may be any one or more of the following:

- The person has some mental disorder such as Alzheimer's disease or other confusional state which makes it dangerous for them to live alone or makes caring for them by the family an impossible task.
- Inability to cope alone either because of physical ill-health or frailty.
- Poverty.
- The client may have been hospitalised.
- Death of a spouse-carer.

Sometimes the client refers themselves, and at other times the referral is made by someone else. Either way, the client should be involved as much as possible in any decision process.

Homes vary in the type of care they can offer. Many of the older homes are unable to cope with the less-able elderly, and also tend to offer a more communal lifestyle. The newer, custom-built accommodation tends to offer more privacy, often allowing the more able residents to cater for themselves.

Nowadays the residents in residential care are becoming increasingly less able and more dependent due to a combination of factors:

- the number of elderly people is increasing (*see* Fig 9.2)
- people are living longer
- the implementation of community care has meant that the elderly are able to live in their own homes for longer
- hospital geriatric beds are being closed to save money
- many private residential homes are unable to offer nursing or psychiatric care
- sheltered housing offers an intermediate stage between living alone and residential care.

In the past the elderly who were no longer able to care for themselves, or had no family to do so, would be put into a residential home or on a geriatric ward in a hospital. This no longer tends to happen, which means those who do go into a home are more likely to need special care.

All homes housing more than three residents have to be registered by the social services department of the local authority. There is no legislation about how homes should be run, but there are codes of practice which should be followed by public, private and voluntary sector homes.

As with all services, there are good and bad residential homes. We can all conjure up the image of the bad home: old people sitting in a circle on regulation-issue plastic armchairs doing nothing; regular mealtimes and bedtimes; communal bedrooms; too few toilet facilities and an unpleasant smell. Unfortunately these places do still exist but they are becoming fewer. The better homes offer as much independence as possible: single bedrooms where the residents can use their own furniture; communal rooms so they can socialise; more adaptable mealtimes; individual decor and a high level of care. With training, it is possible for all homes to offer this standard of care.

The transition from home, a place where you can be yourself and find privacy, to a home, which may lack privacy and intimacy, can be traumatic. Home has memories and contact with the outside world whereas a home has none of these, and the client loses his or her ability to be in charge of their own domain.

Research suggests that many of the elderly prefer to remain in their own home despite many problems as this creates the type of stress that keeps them motivated and aware. To remove this stress by, for example, moving into potentially institutionalised residential accommodation, is likely to create apathy and a loss of drive. This concept of positive stress has enormous implications for those providing Part 111 accommodation.

Institutionalisation, according to some psychiatrists, is caused by:

- treating all residents in the same way
- a strict routine
- a barrier between staff and residents
- not treating residents as individuals.

In the past (and in the poorer type of homes today) it is clear that this type of treatment existed. Today, awareness of such issues has meant that the staff in residential homes take care to avoid bad practice. Homes are designed to allow the residents as much privacy and autonomy as possible while still allowing the staff to keep an eye on them. Even homes where residents have to share bedrooms can provide opportunities for personal space.

Public sector homes

These are funded by the local authority and have to be provided by law (*see* p 121). Their standards vary, but are improving all the time.

Because of limitations such as space, funding and staffing, it is not always possible to provide as much privacy and autonomy as possible. Key services such as catering, washing, cleaning and personal hygiene often have to be centralised. Staff working hours mean that the daily routine may also need to be timetabled. Most homes in the public sector, however, are attempting to provide a high-quality service.

Private sector homes

The overall aim of these homes is to make a profit, but this does not necessarily mean that quality is sacrificed. Indeed, the quality of privately-run homes is generally improving as a greater awareness of the need for professional standards is developed. This is partly due to a demand for value-for-money and partly because of the bad press a small minority of these homes received in the past. The latter problem has, in part, been alleviated by the 1984 Registered Homes Act which set out to raise the standards of care and management in privately-run homes.

Private homes tend to be smaller than publicly-funded ones which often makes them more attractive as they seem more personal. They suggest to many the idea of a small homely set-up, yet statistics show that these homes are just as likely to offer shared bedrooms as publicly-funded ones.

Privately-run homes must be registered with the social services department of the local authority, who should regularly visit the homes in their area and check to ensure they meet the accepted standards of safety, hygiene and client comfort.

The future of privately-run residential homes depends on the amount of disposable income available to the elderly, who are in general a group of people most likely to be on or below the poverty line.

Residential care – factors affecting provision

The planning of such accommodation is complex as many factors need to be taken into account:

- creating a balance between accommodation small enough to provide personal care with one large enough to be cost-effective
- accommodation suitable for the fairly active and for the less mobile
- designing accommodation suitable for those with:
  - —sensory disabilities
  - —mental disabilities
  - —physical handicaps
- the need to create a friendly environment by allowing for personal possessions and as much individual freedom as possible
- the need to allow as much independence as possible. To create a totally safe environment means minimising risk. A life without risk results in a loss of self-esteem and identity – the consequences of which are frequently seen in many residential homes.

For those needing additional care there are public, private and voluntary long-term residential homes where 24-hour care is available.

There has been a steady shift from public to private provision of long-term residential care of the elderly since the 1970s. This pattern seems set to continue for the following reasons:

- local authorities are the purchasers of care for the elderly rather than the providers
- public and voluntary sector provision is unable to keep pace with increasing demands because of reduced funding
- care of the elderly wards in the NHS are taking in fewer patients for long-term care.

These factors suggest that the increasing need among the old elderly for full-time, long-term residential care will be met by the private sector.

Residential care – an overview

It is very difficult, in the public and voluntary sector particularly and the private sector to some extent, to get away from the fact that many residential homes are impersonal and alienating places. Criticisms that are made include:

- decoratively dull and unimaginative
- signs of neglect, poorly maintained
- institutional atmosphere
- lack of investment in plant and premises
- lack of resources
- lack of privacy, i.e. shared bedrooms and bathrooms
- loss of independence, i.e. loss of financial autonomy as bank books, pension books and income support are taken away; staff being responsible for administering medication; lack of choice about TV viewing or listening to the radio; little opportunity to form sexual relationships
- task-orientated regimes leading to fixed routines, resulting in a lack of personal development and a speeding-up of physical and mental deterioration.

Although these criticisms apply to all sectors, private homes tend to provide a better atmosphere as they are generally smaller.

Private provision Private residential provision is affected by two factors.

1 Market-led factors, meaning the factors needing to be considered in order to make a profit
- there is a definite and steady 'market', i.e. the increasing number of elderly people needing residential care

- the more well-off elderly are demanding a higher level of care and facilities
- the concept of supported villages will demand a high capital investment input.

2 Regulatory factors, which are factors to be considered to ensure minimum standards of care:
- The Registered Homes Act 1984 sets minimum standards for both care provision and for those who provide the care
- The Code of Practice, Home Life, Centre for Policy on Ageing 1984, suggests minimum staffing numbers
- the local authority, having the power to purchase provision from the private sector, will have more control over standards of care.

Public sector provision

Long-term residential care homes, Part 111 accommodation, were first provided in response to the National Assistance Act 1948 (Part 111 – hence the name Part 111 accommodation). Originally, these homes catered for all ages of elderly, but more recently they have been catering for the older, more frail elderly because either they cannot live alone or cannot be provided for by sheltered accommodation.

Residential homes are classified by the DHSS as either:

- category A homes where the residents need extra help and support
- category B homes where the residents are more able.

The trend is, however, for most of these homes to cater for an increasingly dependent clientele with specialised needs due to mental infirmity or physical disability. Clients like these would have little profit potential for the private sector.

Residential homes may be either:

- purpose-built, with the advantage of custom-built facilities for specific needs. Some homes offer units offering specialised care for the mentally disabled elderly.
- converted older buildings which may have character but may not be suitable for frail and infirm clients.

Staffing in public sector homes varies according to the local authority area. However, here is a general outline of staffing.

A three-tiered management structure

1 The officer-in-charge who is responsible for:
- overall running of the home
- staffing
- admissions
- liaising with other agencies
- liaising with health service staff
- policy planning.

2 The deputy officer who is responsible for:
- everyday running of the home
- specific duties such as supervising care assistants, overseeing medication, etc.
- deputising for officer-in-charge.

3 The third-in-charge who is responsible for:
- everyday running of the home
- specific duties similar to the deputy officer's but with less responsibility than that of the second-in-charge
- deputising for the second-in-charge.

General staff

- Domestic staff who do the cleaning. These staff, although not dealing directly with the elderly clients, will still need some training to help them to understand the needs of the clients.
- Care attendants who tend to the everyday physical, social and emotional needs of the clients.
- Volunteer helpers may be involved in support tasks to help the care attendants.

The staff are encouraged to hold regular meetings to discuss residents' progress and to work out individual care plans.

Voluntary sector provision

This may vary according to the voluntary agency involved. Generally, though, these homes are subject to the same regulatory procedures as public and private sector homes. As they have a charitable status, the motive is often altruistic and profit is not an over-riding motive.

In many cases, voluntary agencies are at the forefront in lobbying for client needs and bringing issues to the public's attention. Many voluntary sector residential homes demonstrate examples of innovation and good practice.

Good practice in residential care provision

There seems to be an increasing awareness on the part of all residential care providers about what constitutes good practice in long-term care provision:

- the need to give value-for-money
- an awareness of consumer needs in an increasingly market-led area of provision
- insight into the needs of the residents:
  —independence
  —activities
  —self-esteem
  —choice
  —self-advocacy

—some element of risk and decision-making
—privacy and personal space
—pleasant surroundings
—good facilities and amenities.

These factors are part of good practice in long-term care provision, but cost money to implement, regulate and operate. The wide variety of provision offered by the public, private and voluntary sectors needs to be carefully monitored and co-ordinated to ensure that this variety represents a true choice rather than a confusing mish-mash of separate and unrelated provision.

Health Service provision – care of the elderly units

Once the elderly person is no longer able to be cared for either in their own home or a residential home, they may be admitted to a care of the elderly unit. Depending on the health authority and the age of the patient, care of the elderly patient may be:

- **age-related**, when patients above a certain age, regardless of their health problem, are admitted directly to the care of the elderly unit. The advantages are that the unit can offer:
  —specialised care
  —an understanding of issues such as incontinence
  —additional therapies
  —ease of referral
- **integrated care**, where the patient may be admitted to other wards, but the care and treatment would integrate geriatric and general medical practitioners.

An overview of NHS provision

There are various types of hospital provision which may be used in treating the elderly patient. The three main types are:

- **day hospitals** where the patient can be brought for treatment from any number of health care staff
- **assessment and rehabilitation wards** where patients are brought in for initial assessment of physical, mental and social needs. Treatment may be intense to start with, and some hospitals offer a next stage ward which has an emphasis on rehabilitation. Of the patients who do not return to the community, some die and others will go on to long-term residential care or continuing care units
- **continuing care units** which offer long-term hospital care to patients who are not ready or able to return to the community. It may be that there is no likelihood of a cure, but medical treatment is needed.

There are certain factors that need to be considered when planning hospital care for the elderly:

- There is a reduction in the number of NHS beds available, yet the number of old elderly is increasing.
- The numbers of elderly people being cared for in residential nursing homes has increased dramatically; this suggests that many medical staff don't regard the older patient as being treatable.
- While long-term nursing care of the elderly takes place increasingly in residential homes, funding will not go to the NHS where it could be spent on diagnosis and treatment.

Good practice in care of the elderly units

Care of the elderly units, as well as offering medical care, need to be aware of good practice in caring for the elderly. This includes the need for social and emotional stimulation as well as treatment for the health disorder. The approach to nursing the elderly needs to take these needs into account. However, nursing the elderly patient differs from caring for the elderly in long-term residential homes in that the patient is unwell and less able.

Good practice in nursing includes helping the patient to maintain dignity and independence, while giving them a high standard of medical care. Each patient has a different set of needs, and these must be met by an individualised care plan involving:

- assessment of personal, medical and social needs based on medical history, family details, the home environment and the patient's comments
- planning the care programme based on the information obtained at the initial assessment. This programme will offer a programme of individual care made in conjunction with various staff, with the opportunity for feedback and evaluation
- implementing the care programme
- regular evaluation and re-assessment if necessary.

Caring for the elderly patient also means coming to terms with death. The nurse will need to cope with the needs of the dying patient and the family, which is a great responsibility.

Key points – a summary

- We are all responsible in some way for caring for the elderly, either as friends, neighbours and family, or in a professional capacity.

- The first level of care is similar to that needed by the majority of society: the elderly person is generally healthy and is able to ask for any help needed.

- The second level is supported independence: living in their own home occasionally supported by the caring services.

- The third level is domiciliary care where the health and social services liaise to provide care for the elderly person.

- The fourth level is increased supported care, possibly in their own home or perhaps using day centres.

- The fifth level of care is long-term residential care.

- The standard of community care varies according to the area, the level of funding and local priorities.

- Community care provision can be enhanced by the voluntary and private sector.

- Sheltered accommodation bridges the gap between living at home and moving on to Part 111 accommodation.

- There are some new innovations in sheltered provision. These include sheltered villages offering progressive support to the elderly, plus shops and other facilities.

- Residential care provision shows an increasing awareness of the need to avoid institutionalisation.

- Increasingly, public sector long-term care provision is caring for the frail elderly while private sector provision caters for the more able elderly.

- Private sector accommodation is governed by the need to make a profit and to meet various regulatory factors.

- Care of the elderly units may offer long-term or day care to the elderly. Staff are aware of the need to provide social stimulation and activities as well as health care.

Assignment 9 Co-ordinated provision for care of the elderly

TASK 1:
LOCAL
INFORMATION PACK

Within your area, find out what provision there is for caring for the elderly population.

The following suggestions may help:

- The volunteer bureau may have specific good-neighbour schemes in operation. They will also be able to tell you what other voluntary groups are providing.
- Ask around the group if they are aware of any schemes to help the elderly.
- Think of any local fund-raising activities.

- Check whether there are any local branches for national voluntary organisations.
- List all the local agencies, public, voluntary and private, that provide services to the elderly.

When you have done this, compile the information as an information pack for local people.

TASK 2:
LOCAL PROVISION
– A SOCIAL
WORKER'S VIEW

Arrange for a social worker with special responsibility for the elderly to come and talk to the group about their work.

Ask especially about domiciliary care provision in your area. You may wish to include some of these ideas:

- how involved the client is in the decision-making process
- how frequently, and how, the health and social services liaise about a case
- the level of involvement of the:
  —voluntary sector
  —private sector
  —family
  —friends
  —neighbours
- whether there is day care provision and, if so, what it is and who it is provided by
- whether any provision is charged for
- the type of sheltered accommodation available including:
  —whether public, voluntary or private sector
  —the facilities available
  —a measure of its popularity
  —the level of care provided
- how the decision is made, and when, for the client to move on to Part 111 accommodation
- an outline of the local long-term residential car provision, including:
  —whether public, voluntary or private
  —level of need of residents
  —general facilities
  —staff training.

TASK 3:
QUALITIES
REQUIRED BY STAFF

As a group discuss the qualities needed by the following people:

- an officer-in-charge of a residential home
- a care attendant in a residential home
- a warden of sheltered accommodation
- a nurse in a care-of-the-elderly unit.

10 Problems faced by the elderly

The elderly face various problems in their daily lives, some caused by the ageing process itself and some by the social circumstances which tend to surround old age. This chapter will look at some of these problems.

Elder abuse

Child abuse is quite prevalent in our society, but people are less aware of elder abuse. The caring professionals have been aware of the problem for some time, but the general public don't really know what it is.

The main problem lies in defining the term elder abuse. Child abuse has been well-documented and is therefore well-defined, but elder abuse is only relatively recently being researched.

Generally the term elder abuse encompasses the following types of abuse:

- physical
- mental
- sexual
- monetary
- poor living environment.

The abuser can be friend, relative and/or carer. There are enough incidences of elder abuse for some areas to take the problem seriously and to carry out research programmes.

The SSD and health service staff working on elder abuse have realised that, like child abuse, it is important to liaise with all relevant agencies, including the police. The police involvement will bring awareness that it is a criminal offence which will, hopefully, both deter the abusers and encourage the elderly to report the abuse.

The law as it stands does attempt to protect the elderly person's money and property, but not their mind or body. The law has little power to act unless the elderly victim reports what has happened.

Some changes could be made, however, to help reduce elder abuse:

- Laws are needed to facilitate reporting the abuse; elderly people may be reluctant to do so.
- Some carers may be feeling 'close to the edge' and would benefit from improved financial and mental support. Carers are more likely than the average person to suffer from physical or mental illness.
- Increased professional and public awareness of the problem would enable the abused and abuser to seek help more easily.
- A national strategy, similar to that introduced for child abuse, needs to be implemented.

It is important to remember that not all elder abuse is an intentional and deliberate act; it may sometimes be the result of ignorance. Increased awareness through knowledge could help alleviate the problem, but, as always, costs money.

Safety

The elderly are more likely to have accidents because their senses tend to deteriorate and are less acute. Safety hazards can be found in the home and garden and on the roads; we all need to be aware of the potential dangers so we can take precautions.

In the home

Among the elderly population, the greatest cause of accidents in the home needing hospital treatment is falls (*see* Fig 10.1). For women aged 75 and over, 73 per cent of accidents are the result of falls, while for men aged 75 and over the figure is 66 per cent.

As most accidents are preventable with care and forethought, the elderly and their friends and family need to look around for potential hazards and find ways to make them safe.

Lack of mobility may make the person more likely to have a fall, but there are certain precautions that can be taken:

- Install aids and adaptations if necessary to help the elderly person live their everyday lives. These include stair lifts, hand rails, bath rails, ramps and so on.
- If mobility is a problem, try to get living accommodation on one level as far as possible, i.e. have an upstairs and downstairs toilet to avoid having to use the stairs too often.
- Keep stairs and rooms well-lit.
- Avoid loose rugs and carpets and items of furniture scattered around.

On the road, the elderly are more likely to be involved in accidents. Drivers should be aware that an elderly pedestrian may have a poor sense of hearing or sight and may move more slowly.

The elderly themselves should be encouraged to use crossing points such as a zebra or pelican crossings as flashing lights and beepers help to make it clear when it is safe to cross the road.

Failing senses make the elderly an 'at risk' category in accident statistics. Here are some examples of what could happen:

- Loss of memory means that the elderly person may forget. Typical examples of potentially dangerous situations resulting from forgetfulness are:
  —leaving burning cigarettes that may set fire to furniture or bedding
  —leaving the heat on under saucepans, etc.
  —letting kettles boil dry
  —may walk into the road
  —may forget to have household appliances regularly checked.
- Failing eyesight:
  —falls because they cannot see what they are treading on
  —failure to see an approaching vehicle
  —failure to see warning signs.
- Failing sense of smell:
  —failing to smell gas
  —failing to smell burning.
- Failing sense of hearing:
  —can't hear sounds of approaching vehicle
  —unable to hear warnings.
- Failing sense of touch:
  —may be less aware of being burned when sitting by the fire
  —may have too hot a hot-water bottle resulting in burns
  —may develop hypothermia as they don't feel the cold until it is too late.

	Males					Females					All persons
	0–4	5–14	15–64	65–74	75 and over	0–4	5–14	15–64	65–74	75 and over	
Type of accident (percentages)											
Falls	49	37	23	39	66	48	40	34	57	73	38
Cutting/piercing	5	13	26	21	8	4	10	18	9	4	15
Struck by object/person[1]	17	27	20	12	6	16	24	19	10	6	18
Burning	6	3	3	3	3	7	3	4	3	2	4
Foreign body	6	4	6	5	2	7	4	3	2	1	4
Poisoning	6	1	–	–	–	6	1	–	–	–	2
Over exertion	1	–	2	1	1	1	–	1	1	–	1
Other/unknown	10	15	20	18	14	11	18	20	17	15	17

1 Also falling objects

Fig 10.1 Home accidents treated in hospital: by sex and age, 1988 (Great Britain)
(*Source:* Home Accident Surveillance System 1988, Department of Trade and Industry)

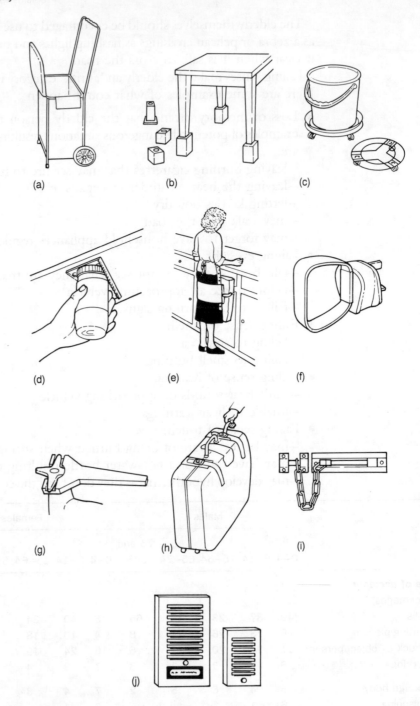

Fig 10.2 Useful household aids
(a) Shopping trolley with a seat
(b) Furniture blocks. If tables, chairs and beds are not at the most convenient height, they can be raised by fitting wooden blocks to the legs. These need to be hollow to a third down so that they can securely support the legs.

(c) Dolly. This is useful for a pail or a hoover and can be pushed along the floor by a foot or a cane.

(d) Jar opener. Fixed underneath a shelf, a jar can be opened by twisting with one hand.

(e) Leg support

(f) Plug handles. These are to make it easier for plugs to be pulled from their sockets.

(g) Tap turner. This will fit any tap in the house.

(h) Suitcase on wheels and a towing handle

(i) Security chain. This, together with a spy-hole, enables people to check who their visitors are before opening the door.

(j) Entry phone. This is not only useful for security, it saves walking flights of stairs to let visitors in.

Lack of money also has an effect on safety. Here are some examples:

- High heating bills in winter may encourage the elderly person to use more dangerous forms of heating such as paraffin heaters. Alternatively, they may economise by using too little heating which increases the likelihood of developing hypothermia.
- The home is more likely to fall into disrepair, especially if the elderly person is unable to carry out the repairs themselves. It is unlikely that they will be able to afford to pay the rather high call-out charges of a repair person.
- Built-in obsolescence means that we now replace many household items, such as kettles, irons, etc., when they become old. The elderly person may be tempted to carry on using a faulty model because the cost of repair or replacement is too great.

With ageing, it becomes more difficult to get out of the bath or some low armchairs. This is a further potential cause of falls.

Keeping the elderly safe is a joint responsibility to be shared by the elderly person and the rest of society. Although we need to be aware of the problems faced by the elderly, they must also be encouraged to take responsibility for themselves.

Hypothermia

Hypothermia is when the body temperature falls below 35°C (95°F). The condition is dangerous and is likely to cause death in the elderly. Three factors can be contributory causes of hypothermia:

- cold surroundings
- failure of the body's temperature-regulating system (homeostasis). The elderly person becomes less aware of feeling cold so, although they feel

cold to the touch, they will not show any of the usual signs of feeling cold, such as shivering
- illness or a fall, or certain drugs such as tranquillisers.

The signs and symptoms of hypothermia are:

- a core body temperature of below 35°C (95°F)
- slow pulse
- stiffened muscles
- vagueness, or even loss of consciousness in severe cases
- slow movements
- pale skin.

Anybody found in a hypothermic condition should be treated very carefully. The first step is to call an ambulance or doctor, depending on the severity of the case. In the meantime, the person should be wrapped in blankets and the room should be gradually heated. Hot drinks and direct heat should never be used as these direct the blood away from the body's inner organs.

Obviously, the best treatment for hypothermia is prevention, such as heating the home in winter. However, there are a number of factors which make the elderly more likely to have poorly heated homes:

- they are less likely than the majority of the population to have central heating
- they cannot afford to draught-proof their homes
- they cannot afford to spend money on heating their homes
- many elderly are unaware of the financial help available to heat their homes.

The DHSS recommended temperature for a house is 21°C (70°F). When the temperature falls below this, there is the risk of hypothermia.

There are various ways of improving awareness of the dangers of hypothermia, both for the general public and for the elderly in particular:

- to have publicity campaigns and give out information to raise awareness
- to find effective ways of informing the elderly themselves both of the dangers of hypothermia and of preventive measures they could take such as:
  —wearing multiple layers of light clothing
  —keeping mobile
  —keeping the room adequately heated
- to make money available, not just for heating bills, but also to insulate and draught-proof homes
- to encourage mobility which will improve circulation.

Generally we all need to be alert to the dangers of hypothermia.

Incontinence

Incontinence can affect the bladder, the bowel or both. Bladder incontinence is the more common of the two, and its incidence increases with age.

Bladder incontinence

There are various causes of loss of bladder control.

- Diseases affecting the part of the brain controlling the bladder, or the nerves to the bladder, can affect the brain's ability to control the bladder. This can be caused by multiple sclerosis, a stroke, etc.
- Stress incontinence is caused by a weakening of the pelvic floor muscles. This is quite common in women who have had a baby, where the muscles may have been damaged or weakened. The bladder may leak urine when the person coughs, sneezes or laughs.
- Infections of the bladder or the urethra may cause temporary incontinence.
- Prostate problems in men may cause continence difficulties:
  —retention of the urine caused by an enlarged prostate gland which prevents the flow of urine
  —increased need and urgency to pass water
  —constant dribbling of urine when the bladder has been emptied.
- Ageing can cause an increasing need to pass water in the night, and these messages from the brain may pass unnoticed.
- Mental disorders such as Alzheimer's disease or other confusional states may lead to loss of bladder control. In some cases, this loss of control may be a response to unwelcome changes such as a move to a residential home.

Clearly it is important that the underlying cause of the incontinence is discovered in order to treat the condition. Some incontinence is temporary and responds to treatment, whereas other types can only be dealt with by careful management.

Treatment and management of incontinence

- Treat any infections with the appropriate drugs.
- Physiotherapy and exercise can help to regain muscle control.
- Prostate problems should be diagnosed and treated.
- Incontinence caused by mental disorders is more of a problem, but should be handled with as much understanding as possible. This is not always easy if the staff, or carer, is overworked and the elderly person is unsure whether they want to go or not.

When as much as possible has been done to treat the problem, the next step is to manage the incontinence. Poorly managed incontinence, as well as resulting in a loss of dignity and self-esteem, is also unhealthy and uncomfortable for the sufferer and unpleasant for those nearby.

There are various ways of managing incontinence:

- Retraining bladder control may be necessary in conditions where the message to empty the bladder is not received. The person should be encouraged to empty their bladder every couple of hours so it doesn't become overfull.
- For those who have trouble reaching the toilet due to disability or loss of mobility, care and consideration need to be given to the practicalities of access to the toilet. This may mean simply installing a commode in the bedroom. Better still, the toilet should be adapted to suit individual needs. More long-term, it may be necessary to move to more suitable accommodation.
- Incontinence aids such as urinals, pants and pads, sheaths, catheters and bed sheets are all available. It is, however, vitally important to be very hygienic to prevent sores and the smell of stale urine from developing.

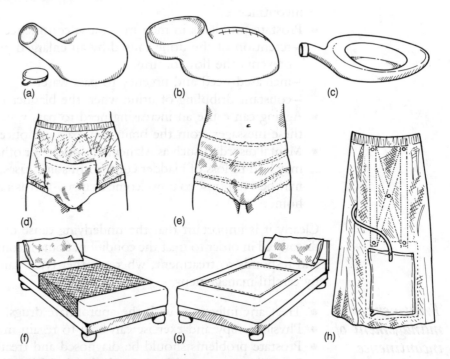

Fig 10.3 Aids for the incontinent
(a) Male urinal. This is invaluable when a person cannot move.
(b) Female urinal
(c) Feminal. This is a polythene bag inserted in a plastic holder.
(d) Fitted incontinence pants. These are made of soft material with a waterproof outside pouch.
(e) Stretch incontinence pants designed to fit any person
(f) Kylie bed sheet
(g) Underpad
(h) Skirt adapted for a catheter and bag

It is important that advice about continence management should be sought to make sure that the best method for the individual is being used. Most health authorities have a continence adviser whose job it is to match the treatment with the individual.

Bowel incontinence

As with bladder incontinence, bowel incontinence may be temporary or permanent. The problem is, fortunately, relatively rare, and can be caused by any of the following conditions:

- mental disorders that render the person unaware of their bowels or the need to empty them
- neurological problems such as a stroke which affects bowel control
- impacted faeces which harden and cause an obstruction and prevent the bowel from emptying. The result is a continual leakage of watery diarrhoea. The impacted faeces may need to be removed manually, often by giving an enema
- diarrhoea may cause bowel incontinence as the sufferer is caught unawares and may not get to the toilet in time
- damage to the sphincter muscle would make it increasingly difficult to control the bowels.

The temporary causes of faecal incontinence need to be treated. Faecal impaction can be removed and diarrhoea treated by drugs. Once treated, the likelihood of the condition recurring can be minimised by eating a suitable diet and maintaining mobility. Conditions needing surgical treatment should be diagnosed and dealt with as soon as possible.

If the condition seems to be permanent, then padded pants may be necessary, but this is seen as a last resort.

The disabled or chronically sick elderly

Disablement in old age can be caused by illness or injury at any point in the patient's life. Alternatively, the person may have been disabled since birth. Chronic sickness is a health disorder which is long-term and unlikely to improve.

Disablement is usually thought of as being physical as with strokes for example, which may leave the person very disabled, but with the opportunity for improvement, given the correct treatment and therapy. Other diseases, such as Parkinson's disease and multiple sclerosis, may be progressive, with the person's condition deteriorating gradually and steadily. Disability can also be mental, as with the various mental disorders associated with ageing (*see* pp 29–37) or social as with communication or emotional problems.

The problems caused by disability and chronic sickness range from inconvenience to being bedridden. The elderly person and the carer need to be aware of the help available as such disorders affect both the sufferer and their friends and family.

Disablement and chronic sickness will have differing degrees of severity and the ways the elderly person is affected will vary. Examples are:

- becoming housebound for various physical and mental reasons
- increasing inability to cope with everyday household tasks
- severe loss of mobility resulting in being chair-bound or wheelchair bound
- becoming an invalid, i.e. bedridden.

The underlying causes of these problems need to be found and then the correct treatment can be started.

For physical disabilities there are a number of useful aids and adaptations available which can be used to make everyday life easier and to maintain independence:

- chairs have been designed to make getting in and out of them easier and safer
- the bed should be the correct design, and there are various pieces of equipment available to maintain safety, keep the bedclothes off the legs, etc.
- aids to mobility such as walking sticks, walking frames, ramps and handrails
- aids to personal hygiene such as bath and toilet rails, shower stools, raised toilet seats, non-slip mats in the bath, tap adaptations, hoists, specially-adapted washing aids, etc.

Ferrule

Fig 10.4 Diagram showing the correct height for a walking stick. It should reach the crease in the wrist.

- dressing and undressing aids such as using Velcro rather than buttons and zips, front-opening clothes and so on
- aids to everyday household tasks such as adapted cutlery and cooking equipment, non-slip plates, one-handed equipment, long-handled equipment for home and garden
- aids and adaptations to help leisure activities.

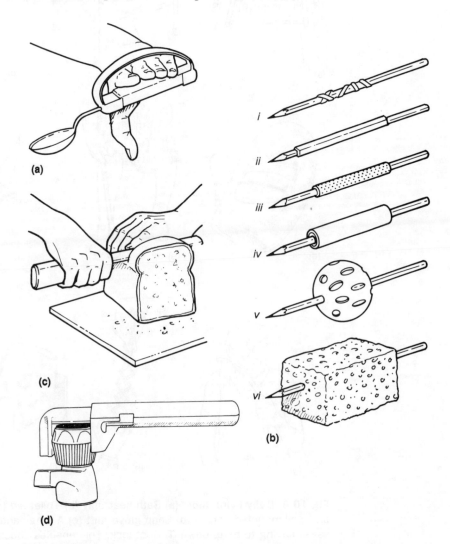

Fig 10.5 Aids for the arthritic
(a) Cutlery. There are many other designs for thick-handled cutlery.
(b) Writing aids. Increasing the diameter of a pencil or pen aids writing so use the following: (*i*) rubber band; (*ii*) rubber sleeve; (*iii*) pimple rubber sleeve; (*iv*) adhesive tape; (*v*) plastic ball; and (*vi*) sponge.
(c) Cutting bread. This method of cutting bread puts less strain on the fingers and wrists.
(d) Tap turner. This device makes modern taps easier to handle for those with stiff or arthritic hands

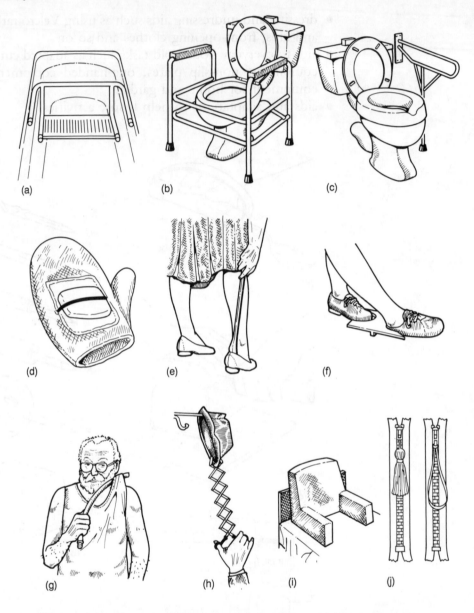

Fig 10.6 Daily living aids (a) Bath seat only (b) Toilet aid (c) Toilet seat raise
and wall-mounted handle (d) Soap glove mitt (e) A long-handled shoe horn
saves having to bend down (f) Boot jack. This enables shoes to be removed
without the wearer having to bend down. (g) Dressing aid. A dressing stick
made from an old wooden coat-hanger will pull straps over the shoulder by the
V-notch. (h) Extend-a-hand. This aid can be adjusted to reach any length. (i)
Bed rest. This is useful when reading or watching television. (j) Zipper pulls.
These make zippers easier to open and close.

Outside the home, there are other ways to make the everyday life of a disabled person easier:

- help with public transport fares and schemes such as Dial-a-bus and Disabled Person's Railcards
- help with wheelchairs
- help with buying a specially-adapted car.

In addition to the many aids and adaptations available, the person needs to find out what allowances they are eligible for from the DSS.

Aids and adaptations, and advice on what may be relevant to an individual, are available from various sources including:

- the Disabled Living Foundation
- voluntary organisations including the British Red Cross Society
- the DSS
- The National Health Service
- the GP.

Figures 10.5 and 10.6 illustrate some of these aids for the elderly.

Caring for the bed-bound invalid is very demanding and it is important to assess whether it is necessary for them to be in bed – this will be done by medical professionals. Sometimes an old person may stay in bed because they are depressed and have lost interest in life. Clearly there are other problems to treat in this situation.

If the elderly person suffers an illness such as pneumonia or a stroke, this will necessitate their being in bed for a certain length of time. There are various problems associated with long-term bedrest. These are:

- stiffening of bones and joints
- muscle wastage
- bed sores
- poor circulation
- loss of independence and general mental deterioration
- increased likelihood of thrombosis and chest infections.

If the elderly person has to spend time in bed, then the care given has to be carefully devised to avoid these problems.

Good practice guidelines for caring for the bedbound elderly patient

Communication is vital so the patient feels involved in the process and is therefore more likely to remain mentally alert. Remember that the patient:

- is an individual
- has a need for dignity and privacy. It is easy to forget this when there are so many tasks to do
- will have changing emotional patterns and may develop symptoms of anxiety and depression

- needs to be kept as active as possible, both physically and mentally
- needs love and affection as well as physical care
- should be respected.

The carer needs support and advice from all the caring services, including the voluntary sector. In addition to this they also need to look after their own needs, and this means:

- eating a healthy diet
- getting regular exercise
- getting plenty of sleep
- sharing the work of caring
- having a social life.

Once the carer and the patient have built up a relationship the nursing process should become easier.

If the patient is to be nursed at home, then there are various issues that need to be considered from the outset.

The sick room will need:

- to be within reach of the bathroom
- to be easy to keep clean
- to have a pleasant outlook
- to be the right temperature
- to be well-ventilated
- to have the right equipment.

Close to hand there should be:

- washing equipment
- a means of communication such as a bell
- lighting.

Bedding:

- should be washable and light
- there should be plenty available for changes
- enough pillows should be made available for a back support
- a waterproof bedsheet is needed if there is a risk of incontinence.

The patient's **clothing** should be:

- easily washable
- light
- adequate for plenty of changes.

Everyday care of a bedbound patient

The type of care given to the bedbound patient, and the attitude of the carer, can greatly affect their rate of recovery. Being a patient can be very demeaning at times and the carer needs to be aware of this and try to make the patient feel as relaxed as possible. There are many, often quite small tasks that the carer may perform during their day-to-day care of the patient which can prevent complications arising, maintain the patient's comfort and aid their swift recovery.

Personal hygiene. The patient should be encouraged to visit the bathroom, but if this is not possible they will need to be washed in bed – the bed bath. This should be done twice a day, not only to remove stale sweat and waste products, but also to make the patient feel better.

It is also important to care for other parts of the body including the mouth, teeth, hair, hands, feet, eyes and nose. Men will also need to be shaved.

Preventing pressure sores. The main danger of long-term bed rest is the formation of pressure sores. These are painful areas where the skin has broken open which, if left untreated, may become ulcerated, infected and eventually gangrenous. Pressure sores are caused by:

- friction of the parts of the body where the bones are near the surface:
  —elbows
  —knees
  —heels
  —ankles
  —shoulders
  —buttocks
  —lower back
  —hips
- chafing in parts of the body where the skin surfaces touch, e.g. thighs, ankles
- scratching irritations.

The problem will be made worse if the patient has one or more of the following problems:

- sweating
- poor circulation

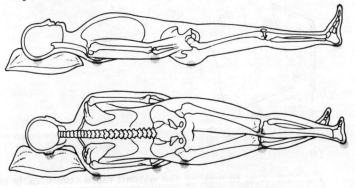

Fig 10.7 Where pressure sores are likely to occur

- incontinence
- rumpled bedding.

It is possible to minimise the likelihood of developing pressure sores by taking these precautions:

- the patient should change position at least every two hours. If they cannot do this unaided, the carer will have to help
- the bed should be kept clean and should be regularly straightened
- the patient should be kept clean to keep sweating to a minimum
- circulation should be encouraged by movement or massage

Fig 10.8 Artificial sheepskin bootees relieve pressure on the heel

(a)

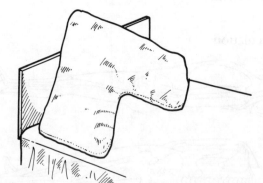

(b)

Fig 10.9 Aids to making the patient more comfortable in bed
(a) Backrest (b) Triangular pillow

- bedclothes should be light
- a bedcradle can be used to keep the pressure of bedclothes off the feet
- a special sheepskin can be bought to place under the parts of the body most likely to develop sores (*see* Fig 10.8).

Encourage rest and sleep as these are necessary for recuperation. This may involve:

- administering pain relief
- making the bed comfortable (*see* Fig 10.9)
- developing a routine
- checking the room is ventilated but not draughty.

Maintain a healthy diet for the patient although they may suffer a loss of appetite. This may involve:

- finding out food preferences
- giving small but appetising portions
- making sure there is enough fibre to prevent constipation
- avoiding indigestible foods
- feeding them if necessary or providing special aids and adaptations so they can feed themselves.

Carry out routine nursing tasks such as:

- taking temperature (*see* Fig 10.10)
- administering medicines
- checking pulse and respiration rates
- observing the patient.

---

1 Take the thermometer. Rinse it under cold water and dry it with a tissue.

2 Shake the thermometer sharply to return the mercury to the bulb.

3 Check that the mercury is below 95°F (35°C).

4 Place the bulb under the patient's tongue. Check the instructions to see how long the thermometer should be kept in place.

Fig 10.10 Taking the patient's temperature

If the patient is immobile, then the carer will need to move them. There are various different methods of moving the immobile patient, either alone or with help, which are designed to avoid damaging the carer's back. Advice on these will be given by the practice nurse or community nurse if asked.

Clearly, if the patient's condition deteriorates to a great extent, then it will be necessary for them to be admitted to hospital where 24-hour nursing and medical care is available.

Death and bereavement

Death is an almost taboo subject today. In the past, when death −and often early death − was a common occurrence, everyone was touched by it throughout their lives. Now, as people live longer and potentially fatal conditions can be cured by medical intervention, we are often unable to come to terms with death.

The role of the carer is to provide for the physical, mental and emotional needs of the patient as well as being aware of the needs of the family and themselves. The dying person, as well as needing nursing care, will need emotional support. There are things that they will be able to discuss with the carer that they may not be able to talk about to family and friends. Some may need the support of religious ministers.

The dying patient goes through recognised stages:

- first of all there is a refusal to accept the fact that they are going to die
- they will then become angry and want to know why they have to be the one to die
- they may attempt to 'bargain' by promising to be good if they can live longer
- there will be depression as the situation is accepted, and they may become introverted
- eventual acceptance of the situation.

Once the patient has died, the carer will need to cope with the grief of the family. Bereavement is a traumatic process, and the carer can be helped by an awareness of the stages of grief:

- denial that the person has died
- anger and resentment that the person has died and left them alone to cope
- 'bargaining' to have the deceased back again
- a period of depression when the bereaved may lose their appetite, become sleepless and lose interest in life. This is when help and support from family and/or professionals is valuable
- acceptance of the death, with an ability to remember the deceased during their life rather than at their death.

The shock of realising that you are going to die, like the shock of being bereaved, follows a pattern. It is, however, important to realise that the feelings are very powerful and, although they will pass in time, it is no help to be told 'you will get over it'. The carer needs to be aware of this, and the importance of undergoing training in coping with death and bereavement cannot be over-emphasised.

Grief is a natural and vital emotion and bottled-up grief can cause untold mental problems. In western society, where death is quite clinical with the majority of people dying in hospital, we seem to have lost touch with many of the rituals which were so much a part of coming to terms with the death – for example, laying out the corpse, watching over the body the night before burial, etc. It is, nonetheless, important that grief is expressed and the carer can help by encouraging this. Many other cultures have retained their death rituals, for example, wailing over the body, and the carer helping the bereaved minority ethnic family must be aware of these cultural differences.

Keypoints – a summary

- Elder abuse is a problem which is becoming increasingly documented. However, more public awareness is needed.

- The problem could be partly alleviated by legislation, support for carers, public awareness and a national strategy.

- The elderly are statistically more likely to suffer from accidents in the home because of mental and physical deterioration.

- Certain precautions can be taken to minimise the dangers of loss of mobility.

- Road accidents could be avoided if drivers were more aware.

- A good many safety hazards are the result of lack of money; the elderly person cannot afford to replace or mend faulty equipment.

- Hypothermia can cause death in the elderly. It is preventable, however, if precautions are taken.

- A person can suffer from bladder or bowel incontinence, although the latter is less common.

- Incontinence causes a loss of dignity. Correct management is important as there are many different causes of the problem.

- Disablement or chronic sickness can drastically alter the person's lifestyle. The carer needs to balance the need to provide care with the need to encourage independence.

- Aids and adaptations are available to help maintain independence for as long as possible.

- Caring for an invalid is very demanding and the carer needs to be aware of their own needs, as well as those of the patient.

- The standard of care can affect the patient's recovery.

- Pressure sores are potentially dangerous but are preventable with care and attention.

- Death is a taboo subject in western society. The carer needs to be able to cope with the needs of the dying person, the family and themselves.

Assignment 10 Caring for the elderly with problems

TASK 1:
ELDER ABUSE

Research any articles on elder abuse you can find in magazines and newspapers. Look particularly at:

- the scale of the problem
- the various types of abuse
- any action that has been taken
- future strategies, if any.

You can find a list of articles by looking in The British Humanities Index, or a similar publication. Your librarian will be able to help.

TASK 2:
LOCAL RESPONSE
TO ELDER ABUSE

Contact your local SSD to find out how the problem is being dealt with in your area. Prepare a list of questions to ask, which may include issues such as:

- whether elder abuse is recognised as a problem in your area
- the rate of incidence of abuse
- staff allocation, i.e. whether all staff are trained to deal with the issue or whether there is a member of staff with specific responsibility
- general strategies for dealing with referrals
- future plans, if any.

TASK 3:
AIDS TO DISABLED
LIVING

Arrange a visit to the Disabled Living Foundation to look at the wide range of aids and adaptations available to help maintain the safety and independence of disabled people. The address is: The Disabled Living Foundation, 380–384 Harrow Road, London W9 2HU.

TASK 4:
HYPOTHERMIA

Look into the various national and local campaigns used to increase public awareness about hypothermia and evaluate their success. The following ideas may help you.

(a) List any national and local campaigns. You will find the information from these sources:

- DHSS
- Health Education Authority } national
- Relevant charity organisations
- DSS
- Health Authority } local
- Volunteer bureau
- Citizens Advice Bureau

(b) For each of these campaigns/information packs, find out:
- the aims
- the methods used to convey the information
- the target audience, i.e. whether for the elderly, their family, professionals or the general public
- the success of the campaign. This can be measured by conducting a survey into public awareness about each of them
- your evaluation of success and any ideas you have that could improve the campaign.

TASK 5:
INCONTINENCE

Arrange to speak with the local continence adviser. If there isn't one in your area, ask who would be best able to talk to you about the issue.

You should ask questions on the following areas:
- the causes of bladder and bowel incontinence
- the size of the problem
- treatment available
- the aids available
- financial help
- what it is like for the sufferer and the family
- help and support available in your area.

TASK 6:
SUPPORT FOR THE
DISABLED ELDERLY

Look into the help and support available to the disabled elderly both nationally and locally.

You should separate your research under these headings:
- physical help, i.e. aids and adaptations
- financial support
- help with mobility
- social support, i.e. help to get out and about and be involved in social events
- advice and counselling support.

You will also need to consider the following factors:

- standard of provision
- availability, i.e. on what basis the help is given; is it based on need, is it means tested, is it for a specific disorder, etc.
- whether the help is short- or long-term
- whether help is statutory or voluntary
- whether standards vary from region to region or area to area.

Finally, as a group, discuss whether you think the help and support available nationally and locally for the disabled elderly is adequate.

**TASK 7:
CARING FOR THE
CARERS**

Arrange to talk to the social workers with responsibility for supporting people who are caring for an elderly invalid in their own home.

Find out about the practical and emotional issues involved and the help and support available for the carers.

**TASK 8:
HOME NURSING**

Home nursing is very demanding as the carer is usually emotionally involved with the patient, and is often present 24 hours a day.

Try to arrange to talk to a professional who knows about home nursing and its demands. You could contact a district nurse or your local British Red Cross branch.

**TASK 9:
THE ELDERLY
INVALID IN
HOSPITAL**

Once the elderly person can no longer be nursed in the home they will be admitted to hospital.

If possible, visit your local care of the elderly hospital unit, or ask a nurse to visit you, and find out about the day-to-day nursing care of the elderly invalid in hospital.

**TASK 10:
BEREAVEMENT
COUNSELLING**

Bereavement is a traumatic process which affects people in many different ways. Carers need to be aware of the needs of the bereaved so they can cope with the situation in a way that benefits both themselves and the bereaved.

Find out about aims and method of bereavement counselling. You can find the information from:
- books
- fact packs provided by relevant agencies
- trained counsellors
- Citizens Advice Bureau
- SSD
- GP or health centre.

11 Getting the best out of life

© John Birdsall Photography

It is very easy when looking into old age to forget that the majority of the elderly live generally healthy and independent lives. This chapter looks at areas which can help to maintain a comfortable old age in terms of both mind and body.

Diet

Most people are becoming more aware of the need to eat healthy foods; with advertisements now promoting the need for high fibre and to avoid salt, fat and sugar in foods it is difficult to ignore the advice.

The old idea that the elderly should eat a light diet of bland, steamed foods has, hopefully, disappeared, but they do need to take certain factors into consideration:

- The metabolic rate slows down as we grow older. This means that we need fewer calories, around 1600–2000 calories a day. The majority of these calories should come from mainly unrefined carbohydrates such as fruit, vegetables and cereals. Refined carbohydrates such as sugar, cakes, biscuits, etc. should be kept to a minimum.
- Eating too few calories means that the elderly person will be less able to cope with illness, injury or stressful situations.
- The elderly have the same everyday needs in terms of fats, proteins and vitamins. They do, however, need to ensure the body's levels of iron, potassium and calcium are adequate.

  Iron is needed to prevent anaemia, potassium to help maintain healthy nerves and to keep the correct composition of body salts and calcium for healthy teeth and bones.

Poor nutrition is potentially dangerous in old age, and is caused by a combination of the following factors:

- lack of money so cheap and filling foods are bought without considering the nutritional value
- ignorance about what constitutes a balanced diet
- lack of interest in preparing food. This is common with widowers who have always had their wife to buy food and cook it for them
- loss of appetite because of:
  —illness
  —loss of mobility
  —mental disorders such as confusion or depression
  —social problems such as loneliness or bereavement
- reaction to drug treatments which may cause nausea or loss of appetite
- overuse of laxatives which result in the food leaving the body before it can be completely digested
- poor teeth so eating is painful or slow
- overeating, perhaps for comfort, or through eating high-calorie foods.

Eating an unbalanced diet can affect health and cause illness.

- Too much saturated fat can cause obesity, heart and circulatory diseases, high blood pressure and many other conditions.
- Too much salt can cause high blood pressure, heart disease, fluid retention and liver disease.
- Too much sugar can cause tooth decay, late-onset diabetes, obesity, and heart and circulatory diseases.

- Too little fibre can cause constipation, cancer of the large bowel, diverticulosis and heart disease.
- Too little vitamin C means that bruises and wounds take longer to heal.
- Lack of iron in the diet may cause anaemia.

Refined foods tend to be high in fats, salt or sugar and are often termed 'empty calories' as they are high in calories but low in nutritional value. They are also comparatively expensive and, although easy to prepare, are best avoided as much as possible.

A balanced diet can help to maintain good health; it can also speed up recovery from physical or mental disorders.

Exercise

Being old is generally no excuse for not exercising to some degree. There are many benefits to be derived from taking regular exercise:

- exercise is a natural relaxant; it helps to reduce stress and depression as hormones are released into the bloodstream
- it helps maintain healthy heart and lungs
- it benefits the muscles and joints, and prevents stiffening
- it lowers blood pressure
- it helps balance and co-ordination.

This does not mean that someone who has previously never exercised should suddenly start an exercise programme. It is always best to consult a doctor before starting to exercise as people have different levels of fitness. Sudden or extreme exercise in the unfit may be dangerous.

The exercises recommended by the Health Education Authority are swimming, walking and keep fit. Many community education departments and publicly-funded leisure centres put on exercise classes specifically for the elderly. (*See* Figs 11.1 and 11.2.)

Money and finances

Finance is one of the main concerns of the elderly. Statistically, the elderly are one of the poorest groups in our society. Although everyone of retirement age is eligible for the state pension, and many people receive index-linked pensions from their work place, funds still often fall short of their needs.

Here is a summary of the possible effects of lack of money on the elderly:

- they are likely to save on heating costs which could lead to hypothermia
- corners may be cut in areas of safety in the home, i.e. electrical and

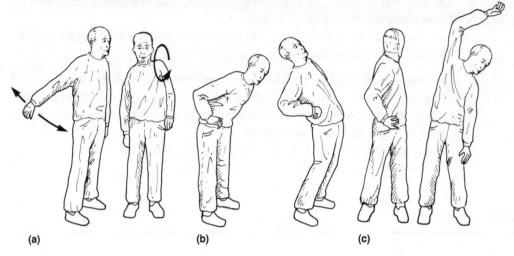

Fig 11.1 Warm-up exercises (a) Arm swings and shoulder rolls **(b)** Body bends
(c) Side stretches

gas appliances may not be serviced, general maintenance may be neglected
- less money may be spent on food, resulting in inadequate nutrition
- their homes are less likely to have certain basic amenities such as central heating, washing machine, 'fridge, etc.
- poverty can cause a loss of status
- the stress resulting from money worries can be too much for many elderly to cope with.

Too little money may ultimately mean that the elderly person cannot live safely and comfortably in their own home.

Why are the elderly more likely to be on the poverty line? The main problem lies in our society which emphasises the importance of those who are working. The result is that non-workers, including housewives and the unemployed, tend to be left out and have a low status in society.

The elderly are not always aware of the financial benefits available to them, or ways in which they can make the most of the money they have. There are three ways this situation can be improved:

- those caring for the elderly in a professional caring capacity should improve their awareness of financial matters so they can refer the person to the relevant agency
- the elderly should be targeted as potential consumers by the banks, building societies and other financial organisations
- there needs to be an improvement in the way the DHSS disseminates information about benefits.

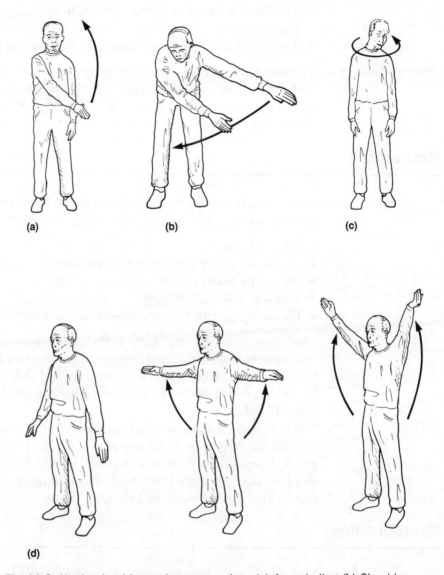

Fig 11.2 Neck, shoulder and arm exercises (a) Arm circling (b) Shoulder swings (c) Neck rolls (d) Arm lifts

To understand the types of benefit available to the elderly is a difficult task as provision and eligibility change at frequent intervals. Here is a basic outline of what Income Support is:

- As a result of the Social Security Act 1986, Income Support was introduced to replace Supplementary Benefit.
- Leaflets giving updates of regulations and amendments can be found in GP's surgeries, health centres, SSDs, walk-in centres, day centres, hospitals, Citizens Advice Bureaux, etc.

- The Income Support Manual details how the system works. It can be found in your SSD, advice agencies and public library.
- The Social Security Commissioners deal with appeals.

The benefits system is very complex and each individual case is different. Although there are leaflets available, the person is best advised to seek professional advice from either the SSD, Department of Social Security Office, Citizens Advice Bureau or relevant voluntary organisation.

Retirement

Retirement is not always looked forward to by the elderly. Since we live in a work-orientated society, retirement can mean:

- a loss of status
- a sense of no longer being a useful member of society
- losing the social contact of work
- losing a 'sense of purpose'
- becoming part of the 'receiving end' of society.

Many people regard retirement as an endless void with too little money to do anything worthwhile. However, it is important for the retired person to continue to feel involved in some way, and this could perhaps be met by taking a course or class that will stimulate the mind and involve meeting other people.

   It is important that both individuals and organisations understand the importance of preparing for retirement so that the mental, physical and social changes do not come as a complete shock. Retirement is not just stopping work, it means planning finances, thinking about leisure interests, considering health issues and housing needs.

Relationships

The elderly have the same need for personal relationships as the rest of society, but little consideration is given to their needs. Magazine articles deal with teenage and adult relationships, but the elderly are largely ignored.

   Why is there this general dismissal of their needs? A number of possible answers include:

- publications dealing with the elderly are usually task-orientated, so emphasise the physical and mental needs rather than emotional ones
- marketing tends to ignore the elderly as they are not seen as potential money-spinners. The result is that there are no magazines aimed at the elderly as a group, they are generally ignored in advertising, and products are targeted at an increasingly young consumer group.
- the elderly are not usually thought of as having an active sex life – many

people assume that sexual relations stop with the arrival of the pension book.

- there are articles covering the problems faced by children caring for elderly parents, but the views of the parent are rarely considered because the targeted readership is the younger person.

The way the elderly are thought of tends to group them together, yet the needs of a seventy-year-old can differ greatly from those of a ninety-year-old.

The present pattern in the elderly is that they are either married or single through the death of a spouse. In the future this pattern will change as the single people or divorcees of today grow old. Perhaps with these changes will come a change in society's attitudes towards the emotional needs of the elderly.

The elderly couple who have had children, seen them grow up, become grandparents and retired, now have extra leisure time. If they are compatible, this is ideal; if they are not, then problems can arise. There is no reason why a happy couple cannot continue to have a satisfying sex life for as long as they wish. There are, however, some physiological changes that take place that need to be taken into consideration:

- sexual arousal of men and women takes longer
- the man's erection is less frequent, takes longer to develop and does not last as long
- the woman's vagina may need additional lubrication as the natural lubricants tend to diminish
- orgasms are less powerful
- loss of libido, which may occur for a number of reasons, may affect either partner.

As with all age groups, sex is a two-way process, so it is important that each partner considers the needs of the other. Most sexual problems can be treated or accommodated.

Relationships with members of the family can cause problems. Families now tend to be more widespread as people move around the country with their work. It can also no longer be assumed that the daughter of the family will care for the ageing parents. The Welfare State should provide for many of the needs of the elderly which in the past were met by the children of the family.

The elderly may have difficulty coming to terms with the fact that they are no longer the ones to give help and advice to their children, but are often in need of help and advice themselves; the roles of parent and child are almost reversed. Problems can arise in situations when the grandparent may try and force advice on childcare, for example, and understanding is needed by both parties.

Relationships are part of the human condition; songs, books and poems are written about them, advice columns are overwhelmed by them, illnesses are caused by them. The elderly are no different except that they may have fewer reserves to cope with any problems that arise.

Sleep and relaxation

The amount of sleep needed varies from person to person, although it is generally accepted that we need less sleep as we grow older. We are controlled by an internal clock which has roughly a 24 hour cycle of sleep and waking. For the majority of us, that means sleeping at night and being awake during the day.

There are two stages of sleep. First we fall into a deep sleep, and after one and a half to two hours sleep we enter a period of lighter sleep when we dream; this is called the Rapid Eye Movement (REM) sleep. The elderly tend to have less deep sleep so often wake up feeling unrefreshed the next day.

The elderly frequently complain of being unable to sleep, although it is thought that they often sleep longer than they realise or admit to. The following factors may affect their sleep patterns:

- physical or mental health disorders
- needing to use the toilet in the night
- drinking tea or coffee, which are stimulants, before going to bed
- drinking alcohol in the evening as it affects the quality of sleep
- lack of exercise during the day
- an uncomfortable bed
- an unventilated bedroom.

People who do have trouble either in getting to sleep or staying asleep may be helped by following these guidelines:

- try to take some exercise during the day, depending on health
- avoid drinking alcohol, tea and coffee before going to bed
- keep the bedroom warm but well ventilated
- have a warm milky drink before bedtime
- do something relaxing before going to bed.

If sleeping is still difficult, then it is probably best to give up trying to get to sleep as this makes you feel annoyed and anxious. Instead, it may be better to get up and make a drink or read a book, and use the time usefully.

If possible, sleeping pills are best avoided as they tend to affect the person's ability to concentrate the next day. As well as reducing the quality of sleep, they may also have certain side-effects and dependency may develop very quickly.

Maintaining good health through preventive health care

Everyone needs to be aware of the benefits of preventive health care. This works on the old adage that prevention is better than cure, so illnesses are best treated by prevention, or by catching them in the early stages, rather than waiting to treat the symptoms.

Preventive health care isn't just the responsibility of the health service, it is also up to the individual to make sure they take good care of their body. Preventive health care includes:

- eating a balanced diet
- not smoking or drinking to excess
- taking regular exercise if possible
- avoiding stress as much as possible
- getting enough relaxation and rest
- having regular check-ups at the opticians and the dentists
- having a regular chest X-Ray
- having a regular cervical smear, although frequency of these varies between areas

- taking advantage of mammograms
- having a regular medical check-up
- having blood pressure checked
- seeking medical advice sooner rather than later.

Preventive health care makes sense, and the increased confidence it can bring may help to keep the body and mind feeling healthier.

Elderly people from ethnic minorities

Until recently, the caring services dealing with the elderly have not needed to address the issues of caring for the elderly from different cultures. However, the proportion of the elderly from ethnic groups will increase, and the caring services will need to be aware of certain issues.

Ethnic minority groups in Britain, although predominantly black and Asian, also include people originating from:

- European countries such as Poland, Italy, Portugal, Spain, Greece, Turkey, etc.
- Iran
- West Africa
- Vietnam
- Hong Kong

Within each racial origin group there may be different cultures, different religions and different politics – within the Asian community, for example, there are many different cultural, religious and political differences. All these can lead to a breakdown in communication.

Communication may not break down simply because there is a language problem; many other factors are involved. Here is a list of some of the ways in which people from different cultures may misunderstand each other:

- There may be a class difference; many people from ethnic groups work in unskilled or semi-skilled jobs so may have problems communicating with middle class caring professionals.
- Different expectations may mean, for example, that misunderstandings about the aims of treatment arise.
- There may be a difference of opinion about treatment.
- There may be a reluctance to share what are considered to be personal problems with a stranger.
- There may be difficulties if the carer is of the opposite sex to the patient.
- Patterns of illness vary between different races.
- The health care professional may use over-complicated instructions or explanations.

Perhaps the greatest barrier to communication is racial prejudice, either conscious or unconscious. The majority of us are, to some extent, influenced by racial stereotypes. It is important to make sure these do not get in the way of effective communication.

There are other aspects that need to be considered when working in a multi-racial society. The following is an over-simplified and brief list:

- Racial inequality is found in these areas:
  —health
  —education
  —employment
  —housing
  Racial discrimination can cause social and psychological stress.
- Cultural differences
- The differing role of the family including:
  —gender differences
  —caring for children
  —caring for the elderly
  —family planning
- Differing views on health care
- Differing diets
- Different religious beliefs.

Perhaps some of the following points could be considered as a means of creating health care provision that meets the needs of all ethnic groups:

- Money should be allocated to ethnic groups so they can set up day centres, advice centres and so on for the elderly. Statistics show that there is little take-up of existing places by elderly people from ethnic minorities.
- Interpreters should be available wherever the elderly may go for advice on health, social services or finances.
- People from ethnic groups should be encouraged to take part in planning provision for the elderly.

Key points – a summary

- It is agreed that a balanced diet can help to maintain a healthy body.

- Poor nutrition can have any number of causes; people caring for the elderly need to find out the root problem.

- Eating a poor diet is a contributory factor in many potentially fatal diseases.

- Exercise can promote a healthy mind and body, and can minimise the effects of certain diseases affecting the joints.

- Before starting on an exercise programme, the person should always consult their GP.

- Lack of money is one of the greatest worries for the elderly; the elderly is one of the poorest groups in our society.

- The elderly often put their health at risk by trying to economise.

- Society needs to make certain changes in the way the elderly are regarded in terms of financial potential.

- The Government needs to make information about benefits more widely available.

- The benefit system is very complex and cases vary, so it is important to stress the need for the individual to seek personal help from a professional agency.

- Retirement is not always viewed with optimism; all too often it is seen as an end – of status, of having enough money, of being useful and of having friends.

- Planning for retirement should start early and should be every employee's right.

- The elderly are not generally regarded as having the same needs as the rest of society when it comes to relationships.

- There is little research carried out into the emotional and sexual needs of the elderly. This may reflect society's views.

- Sexual relationships can continue for as long as it pleases the couple concerned.

- As parents age and their children grow older, their roles are reversed and the parent becomes more dependent on the child.

- It is not unusual to hear the elderly complain that they don't sleep as well as they used to. Introducing a relaxing bedtime routine may help to improve sleep.

- Preventive health care can help to maintain a healthy mind and body. If health disorders are present, early detection can maybe treat the problem before it gets worse.

- Britain is becoming an increasingly multi-racial country. It is important that the caring professionals are aware of the barriers to good communication.

Assignment 11 Making the most of old age

TASK 1:
HEALTHY EATING

A healthy diet is important for the elderly, but a healthy diet needn't be a boring one. Look at the type of foods being served to the elderly in your area. These may include:

- meals-on-wheels
- hospital food
- public sector residential home
- private sector residential home
- voluntary sector residential home
- day centre.

Arrange a visit with the local health service dietician to find out what she or he considers to be the important factors when catering for the elderly.

If possible, then look at as many of the catering services as possible and see how the cooks balance dietary needs with available funding. It would also be useful to find out the opinions of the consumers.

Once you have looked at the various establishments, discuss your conclusions.

TASK 2:
FACTORS
AFFECTING
APPETITE

Look into how these conditions may cause the person to lose their appetite:

- illness
- loss of mobility
- mental disorders
- loneliness
- bereavement.

TASK 3:
EXERCISE FOR THE
ELDERLY

Look at the exercises available for the elderly in your area. These may be provided by:

- community education
- health service
- voluntary agencies.

Find out the following:

- when and how often classes are held
- charge, if any
- how popular these classes are
- whether they are mixed.

Find out also whether there are classes for residential elderly, in either homes or hospital.

TASK 4: **INCOME SUPPORT**	Income support is complex. Collect leaflets outlining the benefits available to the elderly and see the range of variations there are.

Ask a social worker with a special interest in welfare benefits to explain some of the issues to you. Alternatively, you could obtain a copy of the Income Support Manual and work it out for yourself.

TASK 5:
RESPONSES TO
RETIREMENT

The following complaints are often made about the prospect of retirement:

● I will lose my status in society
● I will no longer be useful
● I shall miss my colleagues at work
● There will be nothing for me to aim for any more
● I can't bear the thought of needing charity; I've always been the one to do the giving.

Collect some books and leaflets about retirement and look at these problems in more detail. For each complaint, explain what the person means and give possible reasons for them feeling that way.

When you have completed this, write some guidelines, suitable for both employers and for people about to retire, that outline your ideas about how to prepare for retirement.

TASK 6:
RELATIONSHIPS

Find out what information you can on the elderly and their relationships with the opposite sex, their family and friends.

Evaluate this information in terms of:

● whether it is useful
● whether it is in any way judgemental
● what aspects of relationships are dealt with
● whether the needs of the elderly person are considered.

TASK 7:
SLEEP

Visit the library and find out more about sleep. You may find these headings useful:

● why we need sleep
● the effects of sleep deprivation
● the stages of sleep
● how sleep patterns are disturbed.

TASK 8:
HEALTH SCREENING

Look at these areas of health screening and check that you understand what happens:

● mammograms
● chest X-Rays
● cervical smears

- blood pressure test
- blood test
- urine test.

TASK 9:
ETHNIC AND
CULTURAL
DIFFERENCES

Look at the way your local health and social services have catered for the needs of ethnic groups. You may wish to consider the following:

- whether staff take part in race awareness training
- whether signs are written in more than one language
- whether there are interpreters available
- whether special diets are catered for
- whether there is provision to cater for different cultural views.

Write a brief report on your findings. If you think more could be done, include your ideas in a set of recommendations.

Index